STENDHAL ON LOVE

Book I of II

MaryMarc Translations

4/9/2013

Although Stendhal considered On Love his best creation, not many critics and readers will ever agree with him. Henry James called the book unreadable; others have called it bizarre; and some disconcerting and exasperating. Here's a warning by means of a question: what is the 21st century reader to make of this book? In my estimation, with some patience one can find not only an abundance of wit, but also much hidden wisdom about the mysterium tremendum that is human love. If Stendhal's On Love is considered a failure, then all I can say is that he is in good company, for Aristophanes, Plato, Denis de Rougemont, Ortega y Gasset, Eric Fromm and others also fell short—and no one can say they disgraced themselves. Here's a gem that never fails to give hope to men who search for love: "A requirement of love is that a man's face, at first sight, should show both something to be respected and something to be pitied."

Contents

Introduction by Marciano Guerrero

Marie-Henri Beyle (1783-1842), better known by his pen name **Stendhal**, was a 19th-century French writer. Known for his deep analysis of his characters' psychology, he is considered France's foremost realist writer as is evident in his novels *Le Rouge et le Noir (The Red and the Black,* 1830) and *La Chartreuse de Parme (The Charterhouse of Parma,* 1839).

Stendhal's prose is always as fresh as an evergreen, puzzling and motivating scholars and even contemporary critics to attempt to find the source of such freshness. In his *Journals* (Vol. III: 1928-1939) Andre Gide's has this to say about Stendhal's prose:

The great secret of Stendhal, his great shrewdness, lay in writing spontaneously. His thought charged with emotion remains as lively, as fresh in color as the newly developed butterfly that the collector has surprised as it was coming out of the cocoon. There we find that element of alertness and spontaneity, of incongruity, of

IV

suddenness and nakedness that always delights us anew in his style. It would seem that his thought does not take time to put on its shoes before beginning to run.

In the 20th century, Harvard scholar Matthew Josephson credited Stendhal with anticipating the force of the unconscious mind in human behavior:

> He [Stendhal] was aware of the "irrational" or unconscious elements of the mind long before the later nineteenth century psychologists and the men of the Freudian school arrive on the scene.

About *On Love*

Although Stendhal considered *On Love* his best creation, not many critics and readers will ever agree with him. Henry James called the book unreadable; others have called it bizarre; and some disconcerting and exasperating.

Here's a warning by means of a question: what is the 21st century reader to make of this book? In my estimation, with some patience one can find not only an abundance of wit, but also much hidden wisdom about the *mysterium tremendum* that is human love.

If Stendhal's *On Love* is considered a failure, then all I can say is that he is in good company, for Aristophanes, Plato, Denis de Rougemont, Ortega y Gasset, Eric Fromm and others also fell short—and no one can say they disgraced themselves.

Here's a gem that never fails to give hope to men who search for love: "A requirement of love is that a man's face, at first sight, should show both something to be respected and something to be pitied."

■ ■

VII

This book has met with no success, having been found unintelligible, and not without cause. In this new edition, therefore, the author has tried above all to express his ideas clearly, relating how they occurred to him, and has written a preface and an introduction, all for the sake of clarity. Yet despite all this care, for every hundred readers who have enjoyed *Corinne,* not more than four will understand this book.

Although it deals with love, this little book is not a novel, and above all it is not amusing like a novel. It is simply an exact and scientific description of a brand of folly very rare in France. The conventions, whose sway widens daily, more from a fear of ridicule than from moral purity, have turned the word which serves me for title into something unutterable, something that even means lewdness. I could not avoid using the word, and trust that the scientific austerity of my style puts me beyond reproach on that score.

I know one or two legation secretaries who, on their return, will be able to do me this favor. Until then, I can only suggest that those who dispute the facts I shall relate will kindly pay me no heed whatever.

I may be accused with egotism for the form I have

adopted. But a traveler is allowed to say: "*I* embarked at New York for South America. *I* went up to Santa Fe de Bogota. Relatives and mosquitoes bothered *me* on the journey, and for three days *I* could not open *my* right eye."

The traveler is not accused of being too fond of the first person singular; all these I's and *me's* are forgiven him because to use them is the clearest and most interesting way of relating what he has seen.

It is to be clear and graphic, if possible, that the author of this journey into the little-known regions of the human heart says: "I went with Mme Gherardi to the salt mines of Hallein ..." "Princess Crescenzi said to me in Rome ..." "One day in Berlin I saw handsome Captain L...." All these little things have really happened to the author, who has spent fifteen years in Germany and Italy. But being more curious than susceptible, he has never met with even the mildest adventure, nor experienced any personal emotion of note. If he should be thought proud enough to believe otherwise, let him say that an even greater pride would have stopped him publishing his heart and selling it to the public for six francs, like the folk who bring out their memoirs during their lifetime.

In 1822 the author corrected the proofs of this moral journey, so to say, through Italy and Germany, describing things the very day he saw them, and his manuscript contained a detailed account of all the phases of that malady of the soul called *love*. He treated this manuscript with the blind respect that a fourteenth-century scholar would have placed to a newly discovered work of Lactantius or Quintus Curtius.

When he came across some obscure passage, and to be quite frank this often happened, he always assumed that the fault lay with himself. He admits that he carried his respect for the manuscript as far as to publish several passages that he no longer understood. This would be crazy for anyone seeking public acclaim, but when he saw Paris again after his travels, the author believed it would be impossible to achieve success without stooping to pander to the press. Now if one is going to cringe, one might as well keep it for the prime minister. Since what goes by the name of success was out of the question, the author pleased himself, publishing his thoughts exactly as they occurred to him.

In this regard he follows the example of the ancient Greek philosophers whose practical wisdom is his delight and admiration.

It takes years to penetrate intimately into Italian society. Perhaps I shall have been the last traveler in those regions. After the advent of die *Carbonari* and the Austrian invasion, foreigners will never again be welcomed in those drawing-rooms so full of light-hearted joy. The will see the monuments, streets, and public squares of a town, but not the society; the foreigner will always be suspect, and taken by the inhabitants as a potential spy. Or they will fear he may ridicule the battle of Antrodoco, and at the mean shifts necessary to evade persecution by the ten or so ministers and favorites who surround the prince.

I really loved the people there, and I was able to see the truth. For about ten consecutive months I would not speak a word of French, and had it not been for the disturbances and the activities of the *Carbonari* I should never have returned to France, for I value good-naturedness above all things.

Despite the fact that I have made every effort to be clear and lucid I cannot work miracles: I cannot give hearing to the deaf, or sight to the blind. So people with money and gross pursuits, who have made a hundred thousand francs in the year before they open this book, had better close it again quickly; particularly if they are bankers, manufacturers, or respectable industrialists; meaning: men with eminent positive ideas. The book will be less unintelligible to anyone who has won a fortune on the Stock Exchange or in a lottery. Wealth won in such a way is perfectly compatible with a habit of daydreaming for hours at a time, or of enjoying the emotions stirred by one of Prud'hon's pictures, by a musical phrase by Mozart, or by a certain glance from a woman who is often in your thoughts. People who pay two thousand workmen at the end of every week do not *waste their time* like this; their minds are always bent on useful and positive things. The dreamer I am speaking about is the man they would hate if they had the leisure to do so; the man they would most willingly choose as the subject of their funny stories. The industrial millionaire has a confused notion that such a man would value a thought higher than a sac filled with a thousand francs.

I take equal exception to the studious young man who, in the year during which the industrialist earned his hundred thousand francs, acquired knowledge of modern Greek of which he is so proud that he is already aspiring to learn Arabic. If you have never been unhappy for some imaginary reason *other than vanity,* and which you would be ashamed to hear disclosed in a drawing-room, then kindly leave this book unopened.

I am bound to displease the women who, in those same drawing-rooms, force attention by their constant affectedness. Having on occasion caught some of them in an unguarded moment of sincerity, so surprised were they that they did not know whether a recent sentiment they had expressed was natural or feigned. How could such women judge a description of true feelings? This book has indeed been their pet peeve, describing its author as despicable.

Do you blush, all of a sudden, when you think of

certain things you did when you were young? Have you been silly because you were tender, and do you reproach yourself, not because you look ridiculous in the eyes of all the room, but rather in the eyes of one particular person there? At twenty-six, did you in good faith fall in love with a woman who loved another? Or again —but the case is so rare that I hardly dare quote it for fear of falling into unintelligibility again, as I did in the first edition— did you perhaps, as you entered the drawing-room where the woman you believed you loved was, think of nothing but to read in her eyes what she thought of you at that moment, so that you held no thought for expressing your love for her through your own glances? These are the antecedents I require in my readers. It is the description of many of these delicate and rare feelings that has seemed obscure to men with positive ideas. What could I do to be lucid in their eyes? Perhaps announce a fifty-cent rise in price, or an alteration to the customs tariffs of Colombia.[1]

This book explains simply, rationally, and, so to speak, mathematically, the various feelings which succeed each other to become, in their entirety, the passion called love.

Imagine a fairly complex geometrical figure drawn in chalk upon a large blackboard. Well, I am going to explain this figure, but a necessary condition is that it should already be there on the board; I cannot draw it myself. It is this inability that makes it so difficult to write a book about love which is not a novel. The reader needs more than mere intelligence to follow a philosophical analysis of this sentiment with interest; it is absolutely imperative that he should have seen love. Now where can one *see* a passion? Here is a source of obscurity that I will never discern.

Love is like what we call in the heavens the Milky Way: a shining mass made of millions of little stars, many of them nebulae. Four or five hundred of the small successive feelings —so difficult to recognize— that go to make up love have been noted in books, but only the more obvious ones are there. Among the many errors is that of mistaking the lesser lights for the greater ones. The best of these books, such as *La Nouvelle Heloise,* the novels of Madame Cottin, the *Letters* of Mademoiselle Lespinasse, and *Manon Lescaut,* have been written in France, a country where the plant called love is chronically afraid of ridicule, stifled by the demands of the *national* passion —vanity— that hardly ever grows to its full height.

What sort of knowledge of love can be gained from novels? When you have seen it described in a hundred bestsellers but have never felt it, is it worth coming to this book to find an explanation of its madness? Like an echo I reply: "It's madness!"

Poor disabused young woman, would you like once

again to relive what engrossed you so much a few years ago, something you dared not mention to a soul, and which nearly cost you your honor? It is for you I have re-written this book and tried to make it clearer. When you have read it, never speak of it without a slight sneer, and thrust it into your lemon-wood bookcase behind the other books; I should even leave a few pages uncut, if I were you.

But the imperfect being that imagines himself a philosopher will leave more than a few pages uncut because he has always been a stranger to the mad emotion that can make a week's happiness depend on one glance. Others, as they get older, exert their vanity to extremes to forget that they could once be so humble as to court a woman and so expose themselves to the humiliation of being refused; they will loath this book. Among the many intelligent people who have condemned this book for various reasons —but always in anger— the only ones I deemed ridiculous were the men whose double vanity could claim always to have been above love's weaknesses, and yet to be gifted with such penetration that they could judge *a priori* the exactness of a philosophical treatise which is simply a detailed description of these same weaknesses.

People of grave disposition, who enjoy a reputation for unromantic wisdom, are much more likely to understand a novel, however passionate, than a philosophical work in which the author coldly describes the various phases of the disease of the soul called *love*. They are moved in some way by a novel, but when it comes to a philosophical treatise these wise guys are like blind men asking someone to read them a description of the pictures in the Museum, and saying to the author: "You must admit that your work is terribly obscure." And what if these blind men are intelligent, long recognized as such, and convinced of their own clear-sightedness? The author gets a rough passage. This is just what happened to this writer over the first edition. Several copies of it were actually burnt by extremely intelligent people infuriated by vanity. I say nothing of the insults, none the less flattering for their fury: the author was gross; he was immoral; he pandered to the public taste; he was a dangerous man, and so on. In countries exhausted by the monarchic system, these epithets are the assured reward for those who choose to write about ethics and fail to dedicate their work to the Dubarry of the day. Literature would be sufficiently blessed if it were not a question of fashion, and if those for whom it is written were the only ones who paid any attention to it. In the days of the Cid, Corneille was just 'my good man' to M. le Marquis de Danjeau. Today everybody thinks himself qualified to read M. de Lamartine, which is great for his publisher, but how hard, how terribly hard for the great poet himself. Today genius caters to people it should not have to demean itself by even thinking about.

The active, hardworking, highly respectable and positive life of a Privy Councillor, a textile manufacturer, or a clever banker reaps its reward in wealth but not in tender sensations. Little by little the hearts of these gentlemen ossify; things positive and useful own them utterly, losing the capacity for that sentiment which, above all, requires leisure, making a man quite incapable of any rational and consecutive tasks.

The whole purpose of this preface is to say that the book which follows it will be grasped only by those who have had leisure enough to commit silly acts. Many people will think themselves offended; I hope they will read no further.

SECOND PREFACE

I am writing for a mere hundred readers, unfortunate, likeable, charming, non-hypocritical, non-self-righteous people whom I wish to please. I know no more than one or two. I have no respect at all for those who lie in order to attract notice as writers. Fine ladies of this sort have to go and read their cook's account-book and the fashionable sermonizer of the moment, whether it be Massillon or Madame Necker, before they can converse with the dispassionate women who are the dispensers of 'notice.' And, take notice, the only way of reaching this exalted position in France is by becoming the high priest of some nonsensical doctrine. I would ask anyone who wants to read this book: "Have six months of your life ever been made miserable by love?"

If you have never experienced an unhappiness other than fear over a lawsuit, failure to be elected a Deputy at the last election, or not being witty enough when you were taking the waters at Aix last season, then I shall go on with my indiscreet questioning, asking you whether within the last twelvemonth you have read one of those outspoken books which force the reader to think. J.-J. Rousseau's *Emile,* for example, or the six volumes of Montaigne? Because if you have never suffered from that weakness of the strong and are not in the unnatural habit of thinking while you read, this book will stir your anger against its author, making you suspect that there is a certain kind of happiness you do not know, though Mademoiselle de Lespinasse knew it,

THIRD PREFACE

I beg the reader's indulgence for the singular form of this *Physiology of Love.*

It is now twenty-eight years since the upheavals which

11

followed the fall of Napoleon, robbed me of my profession. Two years since luck plunged me, fresh from the horrors of the retreat from Russia, into the life of a friendly town where I fully expected to spend the rest of my days; a prospect which delighted me. In happy Lombardy, in Milan and Venice, the important, in fact the only, business of life is pleasure. No one there takes any notice of what the neighbors do, nor cares very much for what happens to anyone else. If you do perceive your neighbor's existence, it doesn't occur to you to hate him. If you exclude the pastime of envy from a French provincial town, what is left? The absence, the sheer impossibility, of malicious envy is the surest part of the happiness that attracts all the provincials to Paris.

Following upon the masked balls during the Carnival of 1820, which were more brilliant than usual, Milan society witnessed five or six crazy events. Although in that part of the world people are used to things which would appear quite unbelievable in France, they talked about these events for a whole month. In this country the fear of ridicule would preclude such strange actions, and indeed it requires all my audacity even to speak of them.

One evening we were speculating deeply on the causes and effects of these extravagances. We were at Mme Pietra Grua's —she is a charming woman who, oddly enough, was not involved in any of these escapades. It occurred to me that perhaps only a year later I should have but a vague recollection of the peculiar facts and the causes we were assigning them. Seizing a concert program, I scribbled a few words in pencil. We intended to play *faro,* and thirty of us were sitting round a green table; but the conversation was so lively that the game was forgotten. Late in the evening Colonel Scotti came in —one of the pleasantest men in the Italian army— and we asked him what details he could contribute about the bizarre events we had been discussing. He told us certain things that he had learned by chance, which cast a different light upon the whole affair.

I reached for my concert program and added the new circumstances.

This collection of details about love has been continued in the same manner, in pencil on scraps of paper picked up in the drawing-rooms where I used to hear the anecdotes. Soon, I began to search for a common law by which to determine the varying degrees of love. Two months later, fear of being taken for a *carbonaro* drove me to return to Paris, intending to stay only a few months; but I have never been back to Milan, where I had lived for seven years.

In Paris I was bored to death, occurring to me to return to that lovable country from which fear had driven me out. Collecting my scraps of paper together, I made a present of the lot to a publisher. But soon we hit a snag: the printer declared that he was quite unable to work from penciled notes, gathering that this sort of draft was quite beneath his dignity. The young printer's devil who brought back my notes looked quite ashamed of the discourtesy with which he had been saddled; he knew how to write, so I dictated my pencil notes to him.

I also realized that for discretion's sake I should have to change all the names, and above all shorten the anecdotes. Though people read but little in Milan, the book would have seemed wickedly spiteful had it fallen into their hands.

So the book that I brought out was unfortunate. I shall be so bold as to admit that in those days I dared to despise elegance of style, and I could see the young apprentice busily avoiding flat endings to my sentences, and sequences of words which sounded odd. For his part, at every turn, he quite happily changed the details of facts that were hard to express. Even Voltaire flinches from things which are difficult to say.

The only value of the *Essay on Love* lay in the number of little nuances of feeling which I begged the reader to verify from his own recollections, if he were fortunate enough to have any. Worse still, I was then, as always, a novice in literary matters. The publisher to whom I had given the manuscript had it printed on poor paper, and the layout was ridiculous. After a month, when I enquired how the book was getting on, he told me: "You might call it sacred, for nobody will touch it!"

It had not even occurred to me to solicit newspaper reviews; it would have seemed ignominious to do so. Yet no work was ever in more dire need of an introduction calling for the reader's patience.

To prevent it from appearing unintelligible from the very first, I had to persuade the public to accept the new word *crystallization,* which was intended vividly to express the assembly of strange follies about the beloved which come to be regarded as true and beyond question.

Back then, steeped as I was in devotion to every slightest detail I had culled from my beloved Italy, I carefully avoided any concessions, any amenity of style that might have made the *Essay on Love* seem a little less peculiarly outrageous in the eyes of men of letters.

Besides, I did not flatter the public at all. It was a time when we were all bruised by our recent disasters, and literature seemed to have no other object than to soothe our wounded vanity. Everything victorious rhymed with glorious, and never a sword unsheathed but was laurel-wreathed. The turgid literature of this period never seems to bother with the exact details of the themes about which it claims to be dealing; it merely seeks opportunities to pay compliments to a people enslaved by fashion, whom a great man called the great nation, forgetting that it was only great by virtue of his leadership.

The result of my ignorance of the conditions necessary for the most modest success was that between 1822 and 1833 my book only found seventeen readers; in its twenty years of existence I doubt if it has been understood by more than a hundred or so curious-minded folk. One or two have had the patience to observe the successive phases of the malady of love in those around them who have been afflicted with it. To understand this passion which our fear of ridicule has been concealing so carefully for the last thirty years, you must speak of it as a disease. Indeed this is sometimes the first step towards its cure.

In fact, only after half a century of revolutions that have monopolized our attention one by one, only after five complete changes in the form and trend of our governments that revolution has begun to affect our way of life. Love, or the most common substitute that uses its name, was all-powerful in France under Louis XV; the ladies of the court chose the colonels, and that was the finest position in the kingdom. Now, fifty years later, the court no longer exists, and the most respected women in the ruling middle-class or the disgruntled aristocracy could not influence so much as the grant of a tobacconist's license in the poorest village.

We must face the fact that women are out of fashion; in our salons, brilliant as they are, young men of twenty affect never to speak to them, preferring instead to hang around some coarse driveller with a provincial accent who talks of *capacities,* while they try to get a word in edgeways. Rich young men make a point of appearing frivolous, to give the impression that they are carrying on the gay life of bygone days, but they really prefer to talk about horses or to play for high stakes in gambling-circles where women are not admitted. A lethal chilliness seems to mark the relationships of young men with the women of twenty-five who have been thrown back into society by the tedium of marriage. Perhaps this may lead some wise souls to welcome my scrupulously exact description of the successive stages in the disease known as love.

The scary change which has plunged us into our present boredom, and which makes us quite unable to understand the society of 1778, such as we find it in Diderot's letters to his mistress Mademoiselle Voland or in the memoirs of Mme d'Epinay, may lead us to enquire which of our successive Governments destroyed our faculty for amusing ourselves and increased our likeness to the gloomiest people on earth. We do not even know how to copy their *Parliament* and the integrity of their parties— the only tolerable thing they ever invented. On the other hand, the stupidest of all their gloomy conceptions, the spirit of dignity, has come among us to replace French gaiety, which is hardly to be found anywhere now except in the five hundred suburban ballrooms round Paris, or in the *Midi* south of Bordeaux.

But which of our successive Governments perpetrated the frightful atrocity of *anglicizing* us? Should we lay the blame on the energetic Government of 1793 which stopped foreigners from camping on Montmartre?, a Government which, in a few years, we shall regard as heroic, and a fitting prelude to the one that, under Napoleon, carried our name into all the capitals of Europe.

We may pass over the well-intentioned stupidity of the *Directoire* as illustrated by the talents of Carnot and the immortal Italian campaign of 1796-7.

The corruption at court under Barras still recalled the gaiety of the *ancien regime,* and the graces of Madame Bonaparte were evidence that at that time we still had no taste for the sourness and arrogance of the English.

In spite of the envious spirit of the Faubourg Saint-Germain, we cannot but deeply respect the method of government by the First Consul and able men like Cretet, Daru, etc.... We cannot therefore blame the Empire for the obvious change which has altered the French character during this first half of the nineteenth century.

I need not press my investigation further; the reader will, on reflection, be well able to reach his own conclusions...

■■

That you should be made a fool of by a young woman, why, it is many an honest man's case. *The Pirate,* Volume III, p. 77

BOOK ONE

Chapter 1 — On Love

I want to seek and fix exactly what this passion is, for which all its sincere manifestations are characterized by beauty. There are four different kinds of love:

1. *Passionate Love.* This was the love of the Portuguese nun, that of Heloise for Abelard, of the captain of Vesel, and of the gendarme of Cento.

2. *Mannered Love*, which bloomed in Paris about 1760, and found in the memoirs and novels of the period; for example those of Crebillon, Lauzun, Duclos, Marmontel, Chamfort, and Mme d'Epinay ...

A stylized painting, this, where the rosy hues blend into the shadows, where there is no place for anything at all unpleasant, since that would be a breach of etiquette, of good taste, of delicacy, and so forth. A well-born man will know in advance all the rituals he must meet and keep in the various stages of this kind of love, which often achieves greater refinement than real love, with nothing passionate or unpredictable about it, and it is always witty. It is a cold, pretty miniature when matched against an oil painting by one of the Carrachi. And while passionate love carries us away against our real interests, mannered love always respects those interests: let's admit though, if you take away vanity, very little will be left of mannered love; the poor weakened invalid will hardly drag itself along.

3. *Physical Love.* You are hunting; you run into a wholesome young peasant girl who takes to her heels through the woods. Everyone knows the love that springs from this kind of pleasure, and however desiccated and miserable you may be, this is where your love-life begins at sixteen.

4. *Vanity-Love.* The great majority of men, especially in France, both desire and possess a fashionable woman, just like one might own a fine horse: as a luxury befitting a young man. Vanity, a little flattered and a little piqued, leads to enthusiasm. Sometimes there is physical love, but not always; often even physical pleasure is lacking. "A duchess is never more than thirty in the eyes of a bourgeois," said the Duchesse de Chaulnes, and the courtiers of that just king Louis of Holland joyfully recall

even now a pretty woman from The Hague who was quite unable to resist the charms of anyone being a duke or a prince. But true to hierarchy protocol, as soon as a prince came to court she would send her duke packing. She was rather like a symbol of seniority in the diplomatic corps!

The happiest version of this insipid relationship is where physical pleasure grows with habit, with memories producing a semblance of love. You have the pricking at your pride and the sadness in satisfaction as the atmosphere of romantic fiction grabs you by the throat, believing yourself lovesick and melancholy, for vanity will always aspire to be grand passion. One thing is certain though: whichever kind of love produces the pleasures, they become vivid, and their recollection gripping, only from the instant of inspiration. In love, unlike in most other passions, the remembrance of what you have had and lost will always be better than what you can hope for in the future.

On occasion in vanity-love, habit, or despair of finding something better, ends up in a friendship of the least desirable sort, but boasting of its *stability,* and so on.[2]

Although physical pleasure, being natural, is known by all, it is only of minor importance to sensitive, passionate people. If such people are put down in drawing rooms or made unhappy by the intrigues of the worldly, they possess as recompense knowledge of pleasures utterly inaccessible to those moved only by vanity or money.

Some virtuous and caring women are almost unaware of the idea of physical pleasure; they have so rarely, if I may hazard an opinion, exposed themselves to it, and in fact the raptures of passionate love have practically erased the memory of bodily delights.

We find that some men are victims and instruments of a hellish pride, a pride like that of Alfieri. These men, who are cruel perhaps because like Nero they are always afraid, judge everyone according to their own model, achieving physical pleasure only when they indulge their pride by practicing cruelties upon the companion of their pleasures. This explains the horrors of *Justine*. Only in this way can these men find a sense of security.

Instead of defining four kinds of love, one might well admit eight or ten distinctions. There are perhaps as many different ways of feeling as there are of seeing, but differences of terminology do not change the arguments which follow. Every variety of love mentioned henceforth is born, lives, dies, or finds immortality in accordance with the same laws.[3]

CHAPTER 2 — About the Birth of Love

Here is what happens in the soul:

1. Admiration.

2. You think, "How delightful it would be to kiss her, to be kissed by her," and so on ...

3. Hope. You see her perfections, and it is at this instant that a woman really ought to yield to the utmost physical pleasure. Even the most guarded women blush to the whites of their eyes at this moment of hope. The passion is so strong, and the pleasure so sharp, that they betray themselves unmistakably.

4. Love is born. To love is to enjoy seeing, touching, and feeling with all the senses, as closely as possible, a lovable object which loves in return.

5. The first *crystallization* begins. If you are sure that a woman loves you, it is a pleasure to endow her with a thousand perfections and you count your blessings with infinite satisfaction. In the end you overrate wildly, regarding her as something fallen from Heaven, unknown as yet, but certain to be yours.

Leave a lover with his thoughts for twenty-four hours, and this is what will happen:

At the salt mines of Salzburg, they throw a leafless wintry bough into one of the abandoned depths. Two or three months later they haul it out covered with a shining deposit of crystals. The smallest twig, no bigger than a tomtit's claw, is studded with a galaxy of scintillating diamonds. The original branch is no longer recognizable.

What I have called crystallization is a spiritual process which draws from everything that uncovers new proofs of the perfection of the loved one.

You hear a traveler speaking of the cool orange groves beside the sea at Genoa in the summer heat: Oh, if you could only share that coolness with *her!*

One of your friends goes hunting, and breaks his arm: wouldn't it be wonderful to be looked after by the woman you love! To be with her all the time and to see her loving you ... a broken arm would be heaven ... and so your friend's injury provides you with undeniable proof of the angelic kindness of your mistress. In short, no sooner do you think of a virtue than you see it in your beloved.

The phenomenon that I have called crystallization sprouts from Nature, which ordains that we shall feel pleasure and rushes the blood to our heads. It also spawns from the feeling that the degree of pleasure is related to the perfections of the loved one, and from the idea that 'She is mine.' The savage has no time to go beyond the first step. He feels pleasure, but his brain is fully occupied in chasing deer through the forest, so that he can eat, keep up his strength, and avoid his enemy's axe.

At the other end of the scale of civilization, I have no doubt that a sensitive woman can feel physical pleasure only with the man she loves.[4] This is the direct opposite of the savage's condition. But then, in civilized countries, the woman has leisure, while the savage is so taken up with his work that he cannot help treating his female as a beast of burden. If the mates of many animals are happier, it is only because the male has less difficulty in obtaining his food.

But let us leave the forest and return to Paris. A man in love will see each and every perfection in the object of his love, but his attention is still liable to wander after a time because one gets tired of anything uniform, even perfect happiness.[5]

This is what happens next to fix the attention:

6. Doubt creeps in. First a dozen or so glances, or some other sequence of actions, raise and confirm the lover's hopes. Then, recovering from the initial shock, he grows accustomed to his good fortune, or acts on a theory drawn from the common multitude of easily-won women. He asks for more positive proofs of affection, pressing his suit further.

He is met with indifference,[6] coldness, or even anger if he appears too confident. In France there is even a shade of irony which seems to say "You presume you're farther ahead than you really are." A woman may behave like this either because she is recovering from a moment of intoxication or obeying the dictates of modesty, which she may fear she has offended; or simply for the sake of prudence or coquetry.

The lover begins to be less sure of the good fortune he foresaw and submits his grounds for hope to a critical examination.

Attempting to recoup by indulging in other pleasures, finds them inane. So, seized by the dread of a frightful calamity he now concentrates fully. Thus begins:

7. The second crystallization deposits diamond layers of proof that say "she loves me."

Every few minutes throughout the night which follows the birth of doubt, the lover has a moment of dreadful misgiving, reassuring himself thinking: "she loves me;" and crystallization begins to reveal new charms. Then once again the gaunt eye of doubt pierces him and he stops transfixed. He forgets to draw breath and mutters, "But does she love me?" Torn between doubt and delight, the poor lover convinces himself that she could give him such pleasure as he could find nowhere else on earth.

The dominance of this truth, and the road to it, with a fearsome precipice on one hand and a view of perfect happiness on the other, sets the second crystallization so far above the first.

The lover's mind vacillates between three ideas:

1. She is perfect.
2. She loves me.
3. How can I get the strongest possible proofs of her love?

The most heartrending moment of love in its infancy is the awareness that you have been mistaken about something, and that a whole framework of crystals has to be destroyed. You begin to feel doubtful about the entire process of crystallization.

Chapter 3 — About Hope

All is needed is a very small quantity of hope to beget love. Even when hope gives way to despair after a day or two, love does not diminish.

In a decisive, bold, and rash person, with an imagination whetted by misfortune, the degree of hope can be even smaller and more fleeting, without endangering love.

If the lover has suffered; if he is sensitive and thoughtful, turning from other women in keen admiration of the lady in question, no ordinary pleasure will lure him away from the second crystallization. He will prefer to dream of the slimmest chance of pleasing her, rather than to receive all the favors of any ordinary woman.

At this stage and no later, mind you, a woman who wishes to crush her lover's hopes should do so cruelly, heaping on his head public insults which will make it quite impossible for him ever to see her again.

Even when the periods between all these stages are

prolonged, love is still possible.

Cold, prudent, phlegmatic people must hope longer and more deeply before they fall in love, and the same goes for elderly people.

The second crystallization ensures that love will last; for you feel that the only alternatives are to win her love or to die. The very notion of ceasing to love is absurd when your convictions are confirmed moment by moment, until the passing months make love a habit. The stronger your character, the slighter will be the impulse to disloyalty.

This second crystallization is almost non-existent when love is inspired by a woman who yields too soon.

When the two crystallization processes have taken place, and particularly the second, which is by far the stronger, the original naked branch is no longer seen by indifferent eyes, because it now sparkles with perfections, or diamonds, which they do not see or which they simply do not consider to be perfections.

When Del Rosso was talking to a former admirer of his mistress, who described her charms in some detail, Del Rosso saw a particular twinkle in the teller's eye, which immediately provided another diamond for his crystalline branch.[7] An idea like this, conceived in the evening, would keep him dreaming the whole night through.

An impromptu remark gives *me*[8] enough dreams to last

a whole night through. I see a sensitive, generous, burning spirit - *romantic*[9] as it is commonly called — who sets above the happiness of kings the simple pleasure of walking alone with her lover at midnight in a secluded wood.

Del Rosso would say that my mistress is a prude; I think his is a harlot.

Chapter 4 — Stages of Love

In the unattached heart of a girl who is living in a secluded chateau in the depths of the country the least bit of surprise can lead to a mild admiration. When this is followed by even the slimmest hope, admiration leads to love and crystallization.

This kind of love is rather fun at first.

Surprise and hope are powerfully supported by the need for love and the melancholy which characterize the sixteen-year old. It is so pedestrian to think that sixteen is an age which thirsts for love and is not excessively particular about what beverage chance may provide.

The seven stages of love, then, are as follows:

1. Admiration.
2. How delightful... etc
3. Hope.
4. The birth of love.

5. First crystallization.

6. Doubt creeps in ...

7. Second crystallization.

The interval between 1 and 2 may be a year. Between 2 and 3 it may be a month; unless hope follows closely stage 2 is imperceptibly given up, as causing unhappiness; 3 leads to 4 in a twinkling. There is no interval between 4 and 5; only intimacy could possibly come between them.

Depending on the impetuousness and habitual boldness of the individual, several days may elapse between 5 and 6. There is no interval between 6 and 7.

Chapter 5 — Love is like a fever

Man isn't free to prevent himself from doing what gives him greater pleasure than any other action.[10]

Love is like a fever which comes and goes freely, unconcerned with the will. In this respect mannered love differs from passionate love. The charms of your beloved are not a matter of self-congratulation, except as a stroke of luck.

Finally, there are no age limits for love. Look at Madame du Deffand's infatuation with the boorish Horace Walpole, or the more recent and certainly pleasanter example in Paris itself.

The embarrassing consequences of grand passion are

the only proofs I will accept in evidence of its existence. Shyness, for instance, is a proof of love; I do *not* mean the awkward shame of a boy leaving school.

Chapter 6 — The Salzburg Bough

Crystallization goes on throughout love almost without a break. The process takes place as follows: whenever all is not well between you and your beloved, you crystallize out an *imaginary solution*. Only through imagination can you be sure that your beloved is perfect in any given way. After intimacy, ever-resurgent fears are lulled by more real solutions. As a result happiness never stays the same, except in its origin, bringing forth every day a new blossom.

If your beloved gives way to her passion and commits the grave error of removing your fear by the intensity of her response,[11] then crystallization stops for a moment, but what love loses in intensity —its fears, that is— it compensates with the charm of complete abandon and infinite trust, becoming a gentle habit which softens the hardships of life, giving new interest to its enjoyment.

Should she leave you, crystallization begins again. And every act of admiration, the sight of every happiness she could give you, and whose existence you had forgotten, will end in this searing reflection: "I shall never know that joy again, and it is through my fault that I have lost it!"

It is no use seeking consolation in pleasures of another sort; they turn to dust and ashes.

Your imagination can paint a physical picture for you, and take you hunting on a swift horse through Devon woods;[12] but simultaneously you'll be aware that you could find no pleasure in it. This is the optical illusion which leads to the fatal pistol shot.

Gambling also has its crystallization process, as you envision the use you will make of the money you hope to win.

The intrigues at court, so much mourned by the nobles under the cloak of Legitimism, were fascinating only because of the crystallization they bred. Every courtier envied Luynes and Lauzun their swift ascent to affluence; every attractive woman saw herself with a duchy as great as that of Mme de Polignac. No rational form of government can possibly recapture that crystallization. There is nothing quite unimaginative as the government of the United States of America. We have already seen that among their neighbors, the savages' crystallization is almost unknown. The Romans had but a bare idea of it, and then only about physical love.

Hatred, too, has its crystallization; as soon as you see a hope of revenge, your hatred breaks out afresh.

If belief in the absurd or unproven tends to bring the most incongruous people to the top, that is another result of crystallization. It even exists in mathematics (see the Newtonians in 1740), in minds which could not at any given moment grasp simultaneously all the stages of proof in evidence of their beliefs.

Think of the fate of the great German philosophers, whose immortality was so widely proclaimed: their fame never lasted more than thirty or forty years.

It is because we can never understand the whys and wherefores of our feelings that even the wisest men are fanatical about such things as music.

It is impossible to justify oneself at will against someone who holds an opposite view.

Chapter 7 — About the Different Beginnings of Love for the Two Sexes

A woman secures her position by granting favors. Ninety-five per cent of her daydreams are about love, and from the moment of intimacy they revolve about one single theme: she endeavors to justify the peculiar and decisive step she has taken, defying all her habits of modesty. A man has no such concern, but a woman's imagination dwells reminiscing every enchanting detail.

Since love casts doubt upon what seemed proven before, the woman who was so sure, before intimacy, that her lover was totally above vulgar promiscuity, no sooner remembers that she has nothing left to refuse him than she trembles thinking he has merely been adding another conquest to his list.

Only at this point does the second[13] crystallization begin, and much more strongly because it is now accompanied by fear.

The woman feels she has lowered herself from queen to slave, and matters are made worse by the dizzy intoxication which results from pleasures as ardent as they are rare. And then again, a woman at her embroidery —an insipid pastime that occupies only her hands— thinks of nothing but her lover; while he, galloping across the plains with his squadron, would be placed under arrest if he bungled a maneuver.

I should imagine, therefore, that the second crystallization is a good deal stronger in women, because fear is sharper; vanity and honor are in pawn and distractions are certainly not so easy.

A woman cannot fall back on the habit of rational thinking that a man like myself is bound to acquire, working six hours a day at a desk on cold rational matters. Women are inclined, and not only in love, to yield to their imaginations, and to become ecstatic; so their lovers' faults are quickly erased.

Women prefer emotion to reason.

It's quite simple: since in our stupid way we never give them any business responsibility in the family *they never have occasion to use reason,* and so never regard it as of any use.

Indeed they find reason a positive nuisance, since it descends upon them only to reproach them for their enjoyment of yesterday, or to forbid them the enjoyment of tomorrow.

If you were to hand over the running of two of your estates to your wife, I wager the accounts would be better kept than by yourself; and then ... well, you would of course have the *right* to feel sorry for yourself, you pitiable despot, since you lack even the talent to excite love.

As soon as women begin to generalize they are making love without knowing it. They pride themselves on being more meticulous in detail than men, and half the business across counters is carried on by women, who do better at it than their husbands.

It is a vulgarity that when you talk about business with them, you must always adopt a very serious tone.

The thing is that they are hungry for emotion, anywhere and at any time: think of the pleasures of a Scottish funeral.

Chapter 8 — Men suffer secret torments

This was her favored fairy realm, and here she erected her

aerial palaces. *Lammermoor, I*, 70.

A girl of eighteen cannot crystallize so well as a woman of twenty-eight, because she harbors desires too limited by her narrow experience of life to be able to love with passion.

I was discussing this tonight with an intelligent woman who disagrees with me.

"A girl's imagination," she said, "hasn't been frozen by nasty experiences, with the first fire of youth is still in full flame. Quite possibly she will create for herself a dazzling picture of some quite plain man. Every time she meets her lover she will enjoy, not the man as he really is, but the dazzling inner vision she has created."

"Later, when she has been disillusioned about this lover and about other men, her power to crystallize will have been reduced by harsh reality, mistrust clipping the wings of her imagination. Yet, no matter how outstanding the man may be, she can never again form so compelling an image, and will be unable to love so eagerly as when she was younger. And since in love only illusion appeals and she cannot at twenty-eight give her image the sublime and dazzling tones she dreamed of at eighteen, her second love will seem second-rate."

"On the contrary, madame," I replied, "the very fact that there is mistrust, which was not there at sixteen, will give a new color to this second love. For the very young, love is like a huge river which sweeps everything that is in its way, making you feel that it is a restless current. Now a sensitive person has acquired some self-knowledge by twenty-eight; she knows that any happiness she can expect from life will come to her through love; hence a terrible war develops between love and mistrust. She crystallizes only slowly; but whatever crystals survive her terrible ordeal, where the spirit is moving in the face of the most imminent danger, will be a thousand times more brilliant and durable than those of the sixteen-year-old, whose privileges are simply happiness and joy. Later love, though less gay, will be more passionate."[14]

In this conversation (Bologna, 9th March 1820) a point which had seemed to me quite obvious is rebuffed, convincing me more and more that a man is almost incapable of saying anything sensible about what goes on in the inmost heart of a sensitive woman; as for a flirt, that's another matter, for men, too, have senses and vanity.

The asymmetry between the way love is born for the two sexes corresponds with a difference in the nature of hope for man and woman. One is attacking, the other defending; one asks, the other refuses; one is bold, the other shy.

The man questions: "Shall I be able to please her? Will

she love me?"

And the woman wonders: "Perhaps he's only joking when he says he loves me. Is he reliable? Does he really know himself how long his love will last?" This is why many women treat a young man of twenty-three as if he were a child; of course if he has battled through half a dozen campaigns it's a different matter: he becomes a young hero.

For a man, hope depends simply on the actions of the woman he loves, and nothing is easier to interpret than these actions. For a woman, hope must be based on moral imperatives which are quite hard to evaluate. Most men seek a proof of love which they believe dispels all doubt; women aren't lucky enough to find a like proof. It is one of life's misfortunes that what brings safety and happiness to one lover brings danger and humiliation to the other.

In love, men run the risk of suffering secret torments, while women lay themselves open to public jocularity; in the first place women are shyer, and besides, public opinion means much more to them because 'to be esteemed' is imperative.[15]

They have no sure means of winning public approval by disclosing their real selves for a moment.

So they have to be more cautious. Force of habit commands that all the intellectual processes which constitute the birth of love are gentler, shyer, slower, and more tentative in women, having a greater affinity to loyalty, and are without doubt less able to halt a crystallization once it has begun.

A woman on seeing her lover reflects quickly, or surrenders to the joy of loving, but this joy is rudely shattered if he makes the least advance, because then defense and not surrender is the order of the day.

The lover's part is much simpler. He just looks into his beloved's eyes; a single smile will give him supreme happiness, and will never stops trying to obtain this.[16]

A long siege humiliates a man, but ennobles a woman.

A woman in love is quite capable of speaking no more than a dozen words in a whole year to the man she loves. In the depths of her heart she keeps note of the number of times she has seen him; twice he has taken her to the theatre, twice they have met at dinner, greeting her three times when she was our walking.

One evening at a party he kissed her hand; and you will observe that since then she has been careful, even at the risk of appearing odd, to allow no one else to kiss her hand.

Leonore used to say that this sort of behavior in a man was 'feminine love.'

Chapter 9 — My heart

I am trying extremely hard to be *dry*. My heart thinks it has so much to say, but I try to keep it quiet. I am continually beset by the fear that I may have emitted only a sigh when I thought I was stating a truth.

Chapter 10 — Proof

The following story will suffice as proof of the crystallization principle.[17]

A young woman learns that her cousin Edward, who is about to leave the Army, is a worthy young man and is in love with her already because of what he has heard of her, even though they have never met; no doubt he wishes to meet her before declaring his love and asking for her hand. She sees a young stranger at church and hears him called Edward. She can think of no one else; she is in love. A week later the real Edward turns up, and he is not the stranger in the church. She turns pale ... and of course she will be totally miserable for ever if she is made to marry him.

This is what the small-minded call 'one of the follies of love.'

A man shows the greatest kindness and generosity to a girl who is unhappy; being quite virtuous, he could hardly be more attentive. But he wears a shabby hat, and she notices that he does not ride well. She tells herself with a sigh that she could never marry a man like that.

Another man is paying court to a complete good and honest woman, and she finds out that he has suffered from an embarrassing physical misfortune; all at once she can no longer stand the sight of him. Not that she ever had the least intention of giving herself to him, or that his disabilities detract in any way from his wit and pleasant manners; it is simply that crystallization has become impossible.

It matters not whether it be in the forest of Arden or at a Coulon ball, you can only enjoy idealizing your beloved if she *appears* perfect in the first place. Absolute perfection is not needed, but every seen quality must be perfect. In the second crystallization the beloved will appear absolutely perfect only after a few days. It's quite simple. All that is needed is to think of a perfection to see it at once in your beloved.

You see to what extent *beauty* is necessary if love is to be born. Ugliness is never an obstacle. The lover will soon see beauty in his woman regardless of what she looks like, totally indifferent to *real beauty*.

Should he see real beauty, this will promise him one unit of happiness, while his mistress's features, whatever they are like, will promise him a thousand.

Before love is born, beauty is necessary as an

advertisement, predisposing the lover by evoking praise of the person to be loved. If you admire strongly enough, the least spark of hope will turn it into love.

In *mannered love,* and perhaps in the first five minutes of *passionate love*, a woman taking a lover will care more for the way other women see him than with the way she sees him herself.

Here resides the reason for the success of princes and officers.[18]

Even in his old age, the pretty women at court were in love with Louis XIV.

One must take care not to let hope run free before making sure that admiration exists. Otherwise you would achieve only an insipid flatness quite incompatible with love, or something whose only cure would be in a challenge to your self-esteem.

We have no sympathy with stupidity or with the smile for each and every one. That's why a veneer of sharpness is needed in 'society;' it is the hallmark of manners. Not even laughter blooms on too vile a plant: we scorn too easy a victory in love, and are never willing to set much value on what is ready for the taking.

Chapter 11 — What is beauty?

Once crystallization has begun, you delight in each new

beauty that you discover in your beloved.

But what is beauty? It is a new possibility for pleasure.

Each person's pleasures are different, and often radically so, which explains unequivocally why something that is beautiful to one man is ugly to another. (See the conclusive example of Del Rosso and Lisio on 1st January 1820.)

To determine the nature of beauty, we must investigate each individual's idea of pleasure. For instance, Del Rosso insists that a woman should allow him to risk a gesture or two, smilingly permitting the most delightful liberties; a woman to keep him continually aware of physical pleasure and at the same time giving him the opportunity and incentive to display his particular brand of charm.

For Del Rosso it appears that 'love' means physical love, and for Lisio it means passionate love. It is clearly improbable that they will agree about the meaning of the word 'beauty.'[19]

Because the beauty a man discovers is a new possibility for awakening his pleasure, and since pleasures vary with the individual, each man's crystallization will be tinged with the color of his pleasures.

The crystallization about your mistress, that is to say her *beauty,* is nothing other than the sum of the fulfillment of all the desires you have been able to formulate about her.

Why does one enjoy and delight in each new beauty discovered in the beloved? It is because each new found beauty fulfills a desire. We want her to be sensitive: behold! she *is* sensitive. Then we would have her as proud as Corneille's Emilia and, though the two qualities are probably incompatible, she acquires in a third the soul of a Roman. This is the reason why, on the moral plane, love is the strongest of the passions. In all the other planes, desires have to adapt themselves to cold reality, but in love realities willingly rearrange themselves to conform to desire. As a result, we find more scope for the indulgence of violent desires in love than in any other passion.

Certain general conditions for happiness to exist, conditions which govern the fulfillment of all particular desires:

1. She seems to be your possession, because you alone can make her happy.

2. She is the arbiter of your merit. This condition was most important in the chivalric courts of Francois I and Henri II, and at the elegant court of Louis XV. Under a constitutional and rational government women are entirely denied this means of influence.

3. For a romantic heart, the more sublime the soul of your beloved the more divine will be the pleasure you find in her arms, and the freer from any taint of vulgarity.

Most young Frenchmen of eighteen are disciples of J.-J. Rousseau, and this condition for happiness is important for them.

In the midst of activities so frustrating to the desire for happiness, people lose their heads.

From the moment he falls in love even the wisest man no longer sees anything *as it really is,* understating his own qualities while overrating the least favor bestowed by his beloved. Hopes and fears at once become *romantic* and defiant, no longer admitting an element of chance in things and losing his sense of the probable. While judging by its effect on his happiness, anything he imagines becomes reality.[20]

An alarming sign that you are losing your head is that you observe some hardly distinguishable object as white, and interpret this as favorable to your love; when a moment later you realize that the object is really black, you will regard this as a good omen for your love.

This is the time when, overwhelmed by doubt, you feel great need of a friend; but for the lover there can be no friend. That was well known at court. Here is the origin of the only kind of indiscretion that a well-bred woman can forgive.

The most shocking thing of all about love is the first step: the violence of the change that takes place in a man's mind.

Society, with its brilliant parties, helps love by making this *first step* easier.

The beginning is the change from simple admiration to tender admiration. (What a pleasure to kiss her ... etc.)

A whirling waltz in a drawing-room lit by a thousand candles will set young hearts afire, eliminate shyness; bring a new awareness of strength, giving in the end *the courage to love.* Because in order to fall in love it is not enough just to see a lovely person; on the contrary, extreme loveliness deters the sensitive. You have to see her, if not in love with you, at least stripped of her dignity.[21]

Imagine falling in love with a queen, unless she made the first advances![22]

The ideal breeding-ground for love is the tedium of solitude, with the occasional long-awaited ball; wise mothers of daughters are guided accordingly.

Genuine 'high society', such as was to be found at the French court,[23] but which I think ceased to exist in 1780,[24] was hardly propitious to the growth of love, since *solitude* and leisure were almost impossible to obtain there, and both of these are indispensable for the crystallization process.

Court life trains you to perceive and express a great variety of different *shades of meaning,* and a subtly expressed nuance may be the beginning of admiration and then passion.[25]

When love's troubles are mixed with others (those of *vanity:* when your mistress offends your proper pride, your sense of honor or of personal dignity; those of health, money, or political persecution, etc...) it is only superficially that love increases by the difficulties. Since these troubles hold the imagination elsewhere, they prevent the crystallizations of hopeful love and the growth of little doubts in requited love. The sweetness and the madness of love return when these woes are removed.

Although misfortune favors the birth of love in superficial or unfeeling people, love is also helped by misfortunes which precede it, with the imagination recoiling from the outside world which offers only sad pictures, throws itself —the imagination— wholeheartedly into the task of crystallization.

Chapter 14 — Loving passionately

Many people will disagree with what I have to say now, but I shall limit myself to addressing those who have been, shall I say, unhappy enough to love passionately for many years, unrequitedly and against hopeless odds.

The sight of anything of extreme beauty, in nature or the arts, makes you think instantly of your beloved. This is because, on the principle of the bejeweled bough in the Salzburg mine, everything sublime and beautiful becomes a part of your beloved's beauty and the unexpected reminder of happiness fills your eyes with tears on the instant. In this way a love of the beautiful, and love itself, inspire each other.

One of life's misfortunes is that one cannot recall clearly the happiness of seeing and speaking to the beloved. Apparently you become too emotionally upset to notice the cause of the circumstances. You are aware only of your own feelings, perhaps because you cannot wear out these pleasures by deliberate recollection that they are so strongly renewed by anything which diverts you from the sacred inner contemplation of your beloved and recalls her more vividly by some new relevance.[26]

A burnt-out old architect used to meet Leonore evening after evening in society. In the course of conversation and without paying much attention to what I was saying,[27] one day I waxed eloquent in his praise. She laughed at me, and I was too timid to tell her it was because he saw *her* every evening.

This feeling is so overwhelming that it extends even to

an old enemy of mine who is often with Leonore. Whenever I see this other woman, though I very much want to hate her, I cannot, simply because she recalls Leonore so strongly to my mind.

You might say that by some strange quirk of the heart, your beloved transmits more charm to her surroundings than she herself possesses. The picture of a distant town[28] where you once glimpsed her for a moment throws you into a deeper and sweeter reverie than even her actual presence could evoke. This is because of the adversities you have suffered.

The reverie of love defies all attempts to record it. I find that I can re-read a good novel every three years and enjoy it as much every time. It arouses feelings in me which are related to whatever tender interest engaged me at the time, or, even if it makes me feel nothing, it gives variety to my thoughts. I can also listen to the same music over and over again, but memory must not play any part here—only imagination. If you enjoy an opera more at the twentieth hearing, it could be that you understand the music better, or simply that it recalls the occasion when it was first heard.

As for the new light which a novel is supposed to throw on human nature ... well, I am very conscious of my original views and like to come upon the marginal notes which I wrote about them at a previous reading. But this sort of pleasure only holds good for the novel's function of fosgtring my knowledge of man, and not for its chief function of inducing reverie—which cannot be imprisoned in a marginal note. To do so is to kill it for the present, since one begins to analyze pleasure philosophically. It is also to kill it for the future, because nothing paralyses the imagination more than an appeal to memory. If I come upon a marginal note describing my feelings as I read *Old Mortality* in Florence three years ago, I quickly plunge into my life story, comparing my happiness then with now; in a word, I plunge into deep philosophy, bidding a long farewell to the indulgence of tender feelings.

Every great poet with a lively imagination is shy; in other words he is afraid of men because they can interrupt and disturb his exquisite reveries, and he trembles for his ability to concentrate. Men with their coarse pursuits drag him from the gardens of Armida, and thrust him into a fetid mire, scarcely making him notice them without irritating him. It is because he is emotionally nourished upon reverie, and because he hates vulgarity, that a great artist always is so close to loving.

The more a man has the gifts of a great artist, the more he should aspire to titles and decorations as a protective barrier against the world.

Some moments in violent and unrequited love happen that you suddenly think you are not in love any more. It is like coming across a spring of fresh water in the middle of the sea. You no longer enjoy thinking of your mistress, and even though you are prostrated by her harshness you think yourself even despondent to have lost interest in everything. A wickedly depressed blankness follows a state of mind which, despite its turmoil, still sees all nature fraught with novelty, passion, and interest.

This has happened: the last time you saw your mistress you were placed in a certain situation from which, on some previous occasion, you had reaped a full harvest of sensation. For instance, after a period of coldness she shows a little more warmth, and you feel just the same degree of hope, based on those same external symptoms, as on some occasion in the past; though she may be quite unaware of all this.

The imagination finding its progress barred by the dire warnings of memory, and crystallization[29] stops dead.

Chapter 16 — Perfect music and love

In a little seaside village, whose name I do not know, not far from Perpignan, 25th February 1822[30]

Someone impressed upon me this evening that perfect music has the same effect on the heart as the presence of the beloved, giving, apparently, more intense pleasure than anything else on earth.

If everyone reacted to music as I do, nothing would ever induce men to fall in love.

But I noticed last year in Naples that perfect music, like perfect pantomime,[31] makes me think about the worries of the moment, inspiring me with excellent ideas ... At Naples it was how best to arm the Greeks.

Now this evening I must admit that I have the misfortune of BEING too great an admirer of milady L.

And perhaps the perfect music I've just had the pleasure of hearing after two or three music-starved months, despite nightly visits to the Opera, has merely had an effect I already knew: that of inspiring livelier thoughts about my preoccupation of the moment.

4th March, a week later

I dare neither strike out nor approve what I have just written; certainly I wrote it as I read it in my heart. If I seem doubtful about it now, it is because I have forgotten today what I could see so clearly last week.

The habit of listening to music and the state of reverie linked with it prepare you for falling in love. If you are sensitive and unhappy you will get great pleasure from a tender sad melody, not dramatic enough to goad into action, but evocative only of love's reverie. For example, the long clarinet solo at the beginning of the quartet in *Bianca e Faliero,* or la Camporesi's recitative halfway through it.

The lover who has won his lady will delight in the famous duet from Rossini's *Armida e Rinaldo,* which shows so well the little doubts of happy love, and the bits of joy which follow reconciliations. The orchestral passage in the middle of the duet, when Rinaldo is trying to run away, is strikingly parallels the conflict of passions, making the lover feel his heart stirred almost physically by its influence. I dare not tell you what I feel when I hear it; Northerners would think me quite mad.

Chapter 17 — Beauty and Love

In a box at the theatre, Alberic meets a woman more beautiful than his mistress. Let me express this mathematically: this woman gives promise of three units of happiness as compared with his mistress's two. And let us assume that four units might be promised by perfect beauty.

It isn't surprising that he should prefer his mistress, whose features, *to him,* offer a hundred units. Even little facial imperfections on other women, such as a smallpox scar, touch the heart of a man in love, inspiring a deep reverie; imagine the effect when they are on his mistress's face. The fact is, that pockmark means a thousand things to him, mostly lovely and all fully interesting. The sight of a scar, even on another woman's face, will strongly remind him of all these things.

As we can see, *ugliness* even begins to be loved and given preference, because in this case it has become beauty.[32] A man was once passionately in love with a thin pockmarked woman who died. Three years later, in Rome, he was introduced to two women, one as fair as the dawn, the other thin and pockmarked, and because of it she was, shall we say, unprepossessing. At the end of a week, during which he erased her ugliness with his memories, I saw that he was in love with the ugly one. Of course, with understandable coquetry, she whetted his appetite a little, helping the whole process along.[33]

A man may meet a woman and be shocked by her ugliness, but soon, if she is natural and unaffected, her expression makes him overlook the faults of her features. Next, he begins to find her charming, entering his head that she might be loved, and a week later he is living in hope. The following week he has been snubbed into despair, and a week later he has gone mad.

Chapter 18 — Ugliness and love

Something of this sort happens in the theatre to actors idolized by the public. The audience ceases to care whether they are ugly or handsome. Le Kain, in spite of his ugliness, aroused the passions of thousands; and so did Garrick. There were several reasons for this, chief among them that one no longer seeks real beauty in their features and actions, but only a product of the imagination; something accepted as theirs in recognition and memory of all the pleasure they had already given. In the same way a comic actor gets a laugh by just walking on to the stage.

A young woman visiting the Theatre Francais for the first time might easily find Le Kain repelling in the first scene, but he would soon make her tremble or weep, and she would never be able to resist the characters of Tancred[34] or Orosman. If she were still a little conscious of his ugliness, it would soon be eclipsed by the rising enthusiasm of the whole crowd and the nervous tension it produced in her young heart.[35] There was nothing left of ugliness except the word, and indeed not even that, for one could hear women, fans of Le Kain, shouting "Isn't he beautiful!"

Let us recall that *beauty* is the visible manifestation of character, of the moral make-up of a person; it has nothing to do with passion. Now *passion* is what we must have, and beauty can only suggest *probabilities* about a woman and about her poise. But the eyes of your pockmarked mistress are a wonderful reality which makes nonsense of all possible probabilities.

Chapter 19 — *Beauty's has its limits*

Sensitive, intelligent women are sometimes shy and mistrustful, and after an evening out will painfully pass in review what they may have let slip or implied. For such women a lack of good looks in men doesn't matter for long because soon they get used to it and fall in love in spite of it.

Likewise, if your beloved mistress is harsh towards you, her beauty no longer matters. You stop crystallizing, and if a well-meaning friend tells you she is not really very pretty, you almost agree, and he'll think he is well on the way to curing you.

My good friend Captain Trab told me tonight what he once felt on seeing Mirabeau.

No one who laid eyes on that great man ever felt an unpleasant sensation, in other words, ever found him ugly. Carried away by his electrifying words one only noticed — and enjoyed noticing— what was beautiful in his face. Since just about none of his features could have been called *beautiful* by the standards of the sculptor or painter, what one noticed was beauty of another kind[36]—the beauty of expression.

Your attention carefully erased all that was ugly, pictorially speaking, and at the same time focused sharply on the smallest tolerable details: his hair, for instance, his abundant, 'beautiful' hair ... really. And had he had horns on his head you would have found them beautiful.[37]

The nightly appearances of a pretty dancer compel the attention of those blasé unimaginative souls who adorn the circle at the Opera. With her graceful, bold, and quirky movements she stirs physical love, encouraging perhaps the only kind of crystallization they can still manage. In this way a plain Jane, who could not attract a glance in the street, especially from the jaded, can succeed in being luxuriously kept, simply by frequent appearances on stage. Geoffroy used to say the theatre was woman's pedestal. The more celebrated and faded a dancer is, the higher she is rated; hence the backstage saying: 'You can sometimes sell what you can't give away.'

These women derive part of their passion from their lovers, and are very liable to fall in love *from pique*.

Suppose you watch an actress for a couple of hours every night while she plays noble sentiments; suppose her appearance is in no way unpleasant, and you know nothing of her private life, it is then extremely hard not to associate generous or lovable feelings with her. When you are finally admitted to her presence, her features recall such pleasant associations that her real and often poor surroundings glow with a romantic interest.

"In my early youth," said my friend the late Baron de Bottmer, "I was a great admirer of tedious French tragedy.[38] Every time I was lucky enough to have supper with Mademoiselle Olivier, I was bewildered to see that I respected her, speaking to her as if she were a queen. Bless me if I know now whether I *was* in love with a queen or just with a pretty girl."

Chapter 20 — More on beauty and ugliness

Men who cannot love passionately are, perhaps, those who feel the effect of beauty most keenly; at any rate this is the strongest impression women can make on them.

The man whose heart leaps at the glimpse of his beloved's white satin hat in the distance is surprised at his own indifference to the greatest society beauty. When he sees how much others are moved by this great beauty, he may even feel a little sorry.

Really lovely women are less startling the second day. This is sad because it does not encourage crystallization. Since their excellence is visible to all, they are bound to have more fools in their lists of lovers: princes, millionaires, and suchlike.[39]

Chapter 21 — About love at *'First Sight'*

Even the most ingenuous women,[40] if they have any imagination, are sensitive and *suspicious* and mistrustful without knowing it; after all, life is full of disappointments! So everything formal or commonplace in their first encounter with a man frightens their imagination, causing crystallization to be deferred.

In contrast, in a romantic situation love conquers at first sight.

The process is simple: you are surprised, and as a result you ponder over the event that surprised you. You are already half way to the state of mind in which crystallization takes place.

As an example, take the beginning of Seraphine's love affair in the second volume of *Gil Blas*. Don Fernando is describing his flight from the *sbirri* of the Inquisition:

"It was quite dark, and the rain was pouring; I had crossed several alley-ways and suddenly came upon the open door of a drawing-room. I went in, and at once became aware of the magnificence of the place ... on one side I saw a door a little ajar. I half opened it and could see a vista of rooms, the last of which was lighted. I wondered what to do next... Overcome with curiosity I crept forward through the rooms until I reached the light, which proved to be a candle in a gilt candlestick, standing on a marble table. Noticing a bed, whose curtains were partly drawn aside because of the heat, my attention was riveted by the sight of a young woman who lay asleep, in spite of the thunderclap

which had just shaken the house ... I moved a little closer...
I felt overpowered ... While I was standing there, dizzy
with the pleasure of looking at her, she awoke ...
Imagine her surprise at seeing in her room, at dead of night,
a man she had never set eyes on before. She gave a great
start, and uttered a cry ... I tried to reassure her, and went
down on one knee. "Please," I said, "don't be afraid ..." She
called to her maids... A little emboldened by the presence
of her little serving-maid, she asked me with spirit who I
was . . . etc., etc"

Here is an example of 'first sight' which it is not easy to
forget. In contrast, what could be more idiotic than our
custom nowadays of introducing a girl to her 'intended,'
formally and also a trifle sentimentally! Legalized
prostitution—a mere mockery of modesty.

Chamfort relates how, on the afternoon of 17th
February 1790, he attended a 'family ceremony', as it is
called. That is to say, respectable folks, reputedly honest,
had gathered together to witness and celebrate the
happiness of one Mademoiselle de Marille, a lovely, witty,
and virtuous young woman, who was being privileged to
become the wife of M. R—, a sick, repulsive, doltish, but
wealthy old man. She had seen him for the third time that
very day at the signing of the contract.

"What can be said to characterize this infamous

century," Chamfort continues, "it is that such a matter should be cause for rejoicing; that joy should be mocked; and, in the long view, that these same people should behave with icy contempt and heartless prudery at the least imprudence of a lovesick young woman."

What is essentially artificial and predetermined, and which smacks of ceremony or demands *seemly behavior* paralyses the imagination, allowing it to dwell only on the vulgar and irrelevant; hence the magical effect of a joke at such a time. The poor girl, painfully shy and modest during the introduction to her future husband, can think only of the part she is playing, and this is another sure way of stifling imagination.

A far greater sin against modesty is to go to bed with a man only twice seen, after three words of Latin in a church, than to surrender despite oneself to a man adored for two years. But of course I am talking nonsense.

The prolific source of the vice and misery which follow marriage nowadays is Popery. It makes freedom impossible for girls before marriage and divorce impossible afterwards, when they find they have made a mistake —or rather a mistake perpetrated for them— in the choice of a husband. Look at Germany, that country of happy homes, where that charming princess, Madame la Duchesse de Sagan, has just got most respectably married for the fourth time. What is more, she invited to the wedding her three former husbands, with whom she remains on the best of terms. Naturally, this may be overdoing it; but a single divorce that ends a husband's tyrannies can prevent thousands of unhappy homes. The joke of it all is that Rome is one of the places where divorces are most frequent.

A requirement of love is that a man's face, at first sight, should show both something to be respected and something to be pitied.

Chapter 22 — About *Infatuation*

High breeding is usually marked by curiosity and prejudice, and these ominous symptoms are apparent when the sacred flame —the origin of all the passions— has gone out. Schoolboys entering society for the first time fall prey to infatuation. In youth and age, too many or too few sensibilities prevent one from perceiving things as they really are, and from experiencing the true feeling which they impart.

Overly fervent people —loving on credit, if I may put it that way— will hurl themselves upon the experience instead of waiting for it to happen. Before the nature of an object can produce its due sensation in them, they blindly invest it from afar with imaginary charm which they conjure up inexhaustibly within themselves. As they get closer they see the experience not as it is, but as they have made it, taking delight in their own selves in the erroneous belief that they are enjoying the experience. But sooner or later they get tired or making the running and discover that the object of their adoration is *not returning the ball;* then their infatuation is dispelled, and the slight to their self-respect makes them react unfairly against the thing they once overrated.

Chapter 23: About 'Thunderbolts'

That ridiculous expression ought to be changed, but nevertheless the thing 'love at first sight' does exist. I remember the charming and noble Wilhelmina, despair of the beaux of Berlin; she scorned love and laughed at its follies. Her youth, wit, and beauty dazzled the eye, as did her happiness in every way. Immense wealth, in giving her full scope to develop her qualities, seemed to conspire with nature to show the world a rare example of perfect happiness in a person who perfectly deserved it.

She was twenty-three, and had been at court long enough to have rejected the homage of the greatest in the realm. Being held up as a paragon of modest and unshakable virtue, even the most eligible began to despair of ever pleasing her, and aspired only to win her friendship.

One night she went to a ball at Prince Ferdinand's, and danced for ten minutes with a young captain.

"From that moment," she wrote later to a friend,[41] "he was the master of my heart and of myself, to an extent that would have filled me with terror had the joy of seeing Herman left me time to consider anything else. I could think of nothing but whether he would notice me.

"The only solace I can find today is the illusion that I and my reason were overwhelmed by some superior force. Words cannot begin to express the full extent of the chaos into which my whole being was thrown at the mere sight of him. I blush to think of the surging violence with which I was thrust towards him. If, when he did at last speak to me, his first words had been 'Do you adore me?' I should honestly not have had the strength to avoid saying 'Yes!' I had no idea that a feeling could overwhelm one so suddenly and so unexpectedly. Things had reached such a pitch that at one time I feared I was being poisoned.

"Unfortunately, my dear, you and the world know that I loved Herman. Well, he was so dear to me after a quarter of an hour that since then he has not, in fact could not, become dearer. I saw all his faults and forgave him everything, provided he would love me.

"Shortly after I had danced with Herman, the king left, and Herman, who was on royal escort duty, was obliged to go with him. As he left, everything in around disappeared. I cannot describe the depths of empty boredom to which I dropped the moment I could no longer see him, matched only by the keenness of the desire I felt to be alone with myself.

"At last I was able to leave. No sooner was I in my room, with the door double-locked, than I tried to struggle against my passion. I thought I had conquered it. Oh, my dear, I paid dearly that evening and through the days which followed, for the satisfaction of thinking myself virtuous!"

What you have just read is the exact account of an event which was the talk of the day, for after a month or two poor Wilhelmina's unhappiness was so great as to betray her feelings. A long series of misfortunes followed, culminating in her untimely and tragic death, poisoned either by her own hand or by that of her lover. We ourselves couldn't see much in the young captain, beyond that he danced well, was gay, self-assured, radiated goodwill, and consorted with wantons. For the rest, his lineage barely passed muster, and being extremely poor he did not frequent the court.

An absence of mistrust is not enough; there must be a weariness of mistrusting, and, as it were, courage must be impatient with the whims of life. You are unconsciously bored by living without loving, and convinced in spite of yourself by the example of others. You have overcome all life's fears, and are no longer content with the gloomy happiness which pride affords: you have conceived *an ideal* without knowing it.

One day you meet someone not unlike this ideal; crystallization recognizes its theme by the disturbance it creates, and consecrates forever to the master of your destiny what you have dreamt of for so long.[42]

Women who might experience this misfortune are too fine in spirit to love other than passionately. If they could descend to mere gallantry they would escape it.

Since the 'thunderbolt' is the result of a secret fatigue of what the catechism calls virtue, and of the boredom which comes from the monotony of perfection, I imagine it falls most often on those whom society labels good-for-nothing. I very much doubt whether the Cato type has ever brought down a thunderbolt.

If, when you fall in love in advance like this, you have the least suspicion of what is happening, there is no thunderbolt, and this is what makes them so rare.

A woman made wary by misfortune will not experience this soul-shaking upheaval.

The likelihood of a thunderbolt is greatly increased if other people, particularly women, praise the man who is to be the object of the passion.

Some of the funniest adventures in love are the result of the pseudo-thunderbolt. An insensitive woman who is bored can believe throughout an evening that she has at last found love for a lifetime, filling herself with pride at the thought that she is now undergoing one of the great experiences that her imagination had been craving. But the next day she is hard put to it to hide her confusion and avoid the poor unfortunate fellow whom she adored the night before.

Quick-witted people can recognize these thunderbolts, and so profit by them.

Physical love also has its thunderbolts.

Not long ago the prettiest and most accessible woman in Berlin was seen to turn crimson suddenly as we were out riding in her carriage. The handsome Lieutenant Findorff had just gone by. Soon she was deep in thought, looking worried. That evening, from what she admitted at the theatre, I saw that she was crazed, delirious, and could think of nothing but FindorfF, though she had never even spoken to him. If she had dared, she told me, she would have sent for him. Her pretty face gave every sign of the most violent passion, which lasted through the next day. But after three days Findorff made a fool of himself, and she stopped thinking about him. A month later she couldn't stand the sight of him.

I recommend most of you, if you were born in the North, to skip this chapter. It is an obscure dissertation concerning certain phenomena relating to the orange-tree, a plant which only grows, or at least only attains full stature, in Italy or Spain. To make myself intelligible elsewhere, I should have had to *prune* the facts.

I would have done so had it ever been my intention to write a pleasant book. But, since heaven has denied me literary skill, I have only tried to describe (with all the dourness of science, but also with all its precision) certain facts of which I have been a reluctant witness during my prolonged stay in the country of the orange-tree.

Frederick the Great, or some other distinguished Northerner who never had the opportunity of seeing the orange-tree growing in its native soil, would doubtless have disputed, and disputed in good faith, the statements which follow. I have a healthy respect for good faith; I can see the point of it. Since this sincere declaration may savor of pride I shall add an observation:

We each write at random what seems to us to be true, and yet we give the lie to each other. I think of our books as so many lottery tickets; they are really not worth much more. Posterity, in forgetting some and reprinting others, draws the winning tickets. So those of us who have expressed, as best we can, what we believe to be true, are hardly justified in laughing at our fellows, unless our satire has style, in which case there is every justification, particularly for those who write like M. Courier to Del Furia.

After this preamble I will examine certain facts of which I feel sure that Paris has seldom seen the like. But then in Paris —which is, of course, a city above all others— there are no flourishing orange-trees as there are at Sorrento. And it was at Sorrento, the birthplace of Tasso, on the gulf of Naples, climbing up a slope above the sea and more picturesque than Naples itself, but where no one reads *le Miroir,* that Lisio Visconti observed and wrote down the following facts:

When you are to meet your beloved in the evening, the anticipation of such enormous happiness makes the passing minutes quite unbearable.

In a wasting fever you try twenty different chores and as quickly drop them. You are forever looking at your watch, and you think it's wonderful if you can let ten minutes slip by without a look. At last the hour you have been waiting for strikes —and there, on the doorstep, about to knock, you would be just as glad if she were out. You know you would be sorry later, on reflection; but the fact is that *waiting* to see her causes that disagreeable sensation.

This is the sort of thing that makes ordinary people say that lovers are mad.

What has happened is that the imagination has been violently wrenched from the contemplation of happiness, where every step was new delight, and grim reality now has to be faced.

Being sensitive you know very well that, in the contest about to begin as soon as you see her, the least negligence, the least lack of attention or of courage will be punished by a snub which would poison your imagination for some time, and indeed would be humiliating outside the realm of passion, if you were tempted to withdraw there. You reproach yourself for lack of wit or boldness; but the only way to show courage would be to love her less.

In early conversations with your beloved, the mere bit of attentiveness you divert from the crystallization reverie fails to prevent you making the sort of remark which either has no meaning or means the direct opposite of what you feel. Or even worse, you exaggerate your own feelings and they sound ridiculous, even to you. You are vaguely aware that you are not paying enough attention to what you are saying, imposing at once a mechanical control on what you say. But you cannot stop, because silence is an agony when you can think about her even less. You therefore bring forth sententiously a mix of words which do not express your feelings, and which you would be at a loss to recall afterwards. You stubbornly deny yourself her real presence, in trying to be more closely with her in mind. When I was first in love, this paradox in myself made me wonder if it were love at all.

I understand cowardice and the way that soldiers master their fear by throwing themselves into the thick of the firing. I despair at the thought of how many idiotic remarks I have made in the last two years, just for the sake of saying something.

Here indeed is a clear distinction which women can draw between passionate love and mere compliments, between the sensitive and the prosaic.[43]

At these peak moments the one gains where the other loses; the prosaic soul acquires just that hint of warmth which it usually lacks, while the sensitive soul loses its wits from excess of feeling, and from trying to hide its folly, which is even worse. Wholly occupied in attempting restraint, it has none of the *sangfroid* required to take advantage and is therefore utterly routed where the prosaic person would have made good headway. As soon as the too poignant interests of his passion are at stake, the proud, sensitive person loses the gift of eloquence in the presence of his beloved; failure would hurt too much. The prosaic person calculates the chances of success regardless of the painful risk of defeat, takes a pride in his coarseness and laughs at sensitiveness, which for all its intelligence is always too ill at ease to say the simple things which are bound to succeed.

Being sensitive you are far from being able to snatch anything by force, contenting yourself to receive nothing but *charity* from your beloved. If she herself is capable of genuine feeling, you will certainly regret having tortured yourself by talking to her of love. You look shamefaced; you look frozen; you would even look untruthful were it not that your passion betrays itself in other ways. To express moment by moment what you feel so strongly is a self-imposed duty that comes from reading novels, for if you behaved naturally you would never undertake such a painful task. Instead of describing how you felt a quarter of an hour earlier and trying to make this an interesting and coherent story, you have a naive idea of expressing your feelings as they occur. So you do yourself an injury for the sake of a smaller success. What you say lacks the ring of genuine feeling; your memory is in chains, and you say ridiculous and humiliating things under the impression that they are acceptable.

After an hour or so of this confusion you achieve the extremely painful withdrawal from the magical gardens of the imagination, so that you can enjoy the presence of your beloved in all simplicity; but by then it is generally time for you to leave.

All this may seem fantastic, but I can go one better.

A friend of mine loved a woman beyond idolatry. Heaven knows what pretext of lack of delicacy or something —I never learned the details— she condemned him to visit her only twice a month. These visits, so rare and so anxiously awaited, were pinnacles of total madness, and it required all Salviati's force of character to conceal this madness from the outside world.

From the first, the idea that the visit must end shatters the pleasure. You talk a lot without noticing what you say, and what you say is often the opposite of what you think. You embark on convoluted arguments which you have to cut short because they sound silly, as you would recognize if only you could wake up and listen to them. The strain is so great that you give no sign of warmth and love is concealed by its own abundance.

When you were far away from her your imagination was lulled by the thought of entrancing dialogues, and you were in a state of tender ecstasy. So for ten or twelve days you thought you were brave enough to talk to her, but a couple of days before the 'happy' one, fever set in, and grew worse and worse as the awful moment descended upon you.

As you enter her drawing-room, you can but clutch at a

vow of silence to prevent yourself saying or doing the most unbelievably idiotic things. You can also look at her, in order at least to have some recollection of her face. No sooner are you in her presence than your eyes are afflicted as by a kind of drunkenness, and you are seized with a mad impulse to do odd things. It is as if you had split personalities: one to act and the other to reproach you for acting. In some confused way you feel that to concentrate upon the idiocies will cool your blood for a moment, and banish the thought of the end of the visit and the pain of leaving her for a fortnight.

If some old boring person happens to be present, droning out a dull anecdote, the poor lover in his inexplicable madness is all ears, as if he were indeed anxious to squander away these rare moments. The hour of delight he had promised himself passes like a searing flash, and yet he is bitterly conscious of all the little things which tell him how much he has become estranged from his beloved. He is one among a crowd of indifferent visitors, finding that he is the only one who does not know the little day-to-day details of her life. At last he goes, and as he bids her a frigid farewell, he is vexed by the thought of the fortnight which must elapse before he may see her again. Certainly he would suffer less if he were never to see her. He is even worse off than the Duke of Policastro, who used to travel a hundred leagues to Lecce every six months for a quarter of an hour with his adored but jealously-guarded mistress.

It is easy to see from this that *the will* has no control over love. Outraged by your mistress and yourself, how gladly you would rush headlong into indifference. The visit is only worthwhile for one thing: it renews the treasured crystallization.

Salviati's life was divided into fifteen-day periods, and each period was colored by the evening when he was allowed to visit Mme —; for instance, on 21st May he was madly happy while on 2nd June he dared not return home lest he blew out his brains.

I decided that night that novelists haven't dealt suitably with the moment of suicide. "I'm thirsty," Salviati told me quite simply, "I think I'd better drink this glass of water." I did nothing to dissuade him, but said goodbye; then he broke down and began to weep.

Since the utterances of lovers cause them so much anxiety, it would be unwise to jump to conclusions from any single detail of their conversation. Only in chance remarks are their feelings reflected; then the heart itself cries out. Apart from this, one can only draw conclusions from an analysis of the whole pattern of the conversation between the lovers, minding that a person under the stress of strong emotions seldom has time to notice the emotions of whoever is causing them.

Chapter 25 — The Introduction

I cannot but be immersed in admiration at the shrewdness and judgment with which women grasp certain details. A moment later I see them praising folly, moved to tears by mushiness, and gravely weighing mere affectation as a trait of character. How they can be so silly is beyond me. There must be some law of nature I haven't heard about.

Concentrating on *one* quality, *one* detail in a man, they become so taken up with it that they have no eyes for the rest. All their nervous fluid is engaged in enjoying this one quality so that there is none to spare for perceiving others.

I have seen really first-rate men being introduced to highly intelligent women, but it is always the same: a trace of prejudice and the consequences of a first meeting are decided in advance.

Let me be personal for a moment, and I will tell you how the charming colonel La Bedoyere was about to meet Madame Struve from Koenigsberg, a really fine woman. We were all wondering, *'Fara colpo?'* (would she succumb to him?) and a bet was laid. I went to Madame de Struve and told her that the colonel wore his cravats two days running, and turned them inside out on the second day. If she looked, I said, she would notice the vertical creases on his cravat. The whole story was grossly untrue.

Just as I finished, the good colonel himself was announced. The most insignificant little ass in Paris would have called forth more response from the lady. Mind you, Madame de Struve fell in love; she was a sincere person, and there could never have been a light-hearted affair between them.

Never were two characters more fitted for each other. Madame de Struve was accused of being 'romantic', and the only thing that could touch La Bedoyere was virtue carried to its most romantic extreme. It was for her sake that he shot himself, while he was still quite young.

Women are very clever at feeling the imperceptible changes in the human heart, and at discerning nuances of affection or the least flicker of pride. They have a sense-organ for this that men have not; watch them tending a wounded man.

But at the same time they do not see the thing called intelligence, a moral compound. I have seen some of the best women just passing the time of day with an intelligent man (not myself, by the way) while at the same time, and indeed almost in the same breath, they were lost in the admiration of utter fools. I have stood fascinated, like an expert who sees the finest diamonds mistaken for paste, while paste ones, being larger, are preferred.

I argued from this that where women are concerned one must dare all.

When General LaSalle failed, a captain bristling with oaths and mustachios succeeded.[44] The whole of one side of men's qualities must be completely missed by women.

For my part, I fall back as usual on the laws of physics. The nervous fluid is taken up in men by the brain, and in women by the heart; that's why women are more vulnerable. Men can find consolation in having to get down to some important task in their chosen and accustomed profession; women have nothing to console them but idle distractions.

I was exchanging ideas tonight with Appiani, who believes in virtue only as a last resort. When I explained the gist of this chapter he said: "You remember Eponina, who kept her husband alive in an underground cavern so devotedly and heroically? The force of character she showed in keeping up his spirits would have been used to hide a lover from her husband if they had been living quietly in Rome. Strong characters need strong nourishment."

A woman in Madagascar thinks nothing of showing what is most carefully hidden here, but would die of shame rather than exhibit an arm. Clearly, modesty is largely something that is learned, and perhaps the only law invented by civilization which causes nothing but happiness.

Birds of prey hide themselves when they are drinking, because at the moment when they plunge their heads into the water they are defenseless. Considering what happens in Tahiti,[45] I doubt whether we need seek further for the natural basis of modesty.

Love is civilization's miracle.

Among savages and barbarians only physical love of the coarsest kind exists. And modesty protects love by imagination, giving it the chance to survive.

Very early in life little girls learn modesty from their mothers, who teach it very zealously, as if from esprit-de-corps; this is because women are fostering in advance the happiness of the lover they will one day possess.

If a shy, sensitive woman allows herself to say or do, in the presence of a man, something for which she feels she should blush, her embarrassment is agonizing. I am certain that a woman with any spirit would rather die a thousand deaths. If the man she loves takes the slightest liberty, in all tenderness,[46] she has a moment of acute pleasure, but if he then looks disapproving or even does not appear to be carried away with joy, it must leave her heart full of bitter doubts. A well-bred woman therefore has everything to gain by behaving with strict reserve. The game is one-sided; against the trace of pleasure or the advantage of seeming just a little more charming, she has to pit the risk of scorching remorse and a feeling of shame which would blight her love. This is a heavy price to pay for a carefree evening and one of heedless gaiety. For days afterwards she must hate the sight of a lover with whom she has shared 'mistakes' of this kind. It is hardly surprising to find a habit so ingrained, when the least lapse from it is punished so severely by the blackest shame.

As for the purpose of modesty, it is the mother of love; that is enough to justify it. Its mechanism is extremely simple. The heart becomes filled with shame instead of with desire. Desire is thus inhibited, and desire is what leads to deeds.

It is clear that every sensitive, spirited woman —and these two qualities seldom exist apart, since they are cause and effect— that every such woman must assume habits of coldness which are labeled 'prudishness' by those whom they disconcert.

Now this accusation is the more false since it is

extremely difficult to strike a happy medium. If a woman has more pride than intelligence she will soon come to believe that the need for modesty has no limits. Thus an Englishwoman takes offence if certain garments are mentioned in her presence. At a country house she will take care to avoid being seen leaving the room in company with her husband at bedtime and worse still she thinks it an offence against modesty to be jolly in the presence of anyone but her husband.[47] Perhaps it is because they are so peculiar that the English, an intelligent people, are so patently bored with domestic bliss. It is their own fault, so why so much self-righteousness?[48]

Moving swiftly from Plymouth to Cadiz and Seville, I found a different story in Spain. There the warmth of the climate and of the passions resulted in a little too much unconcern for propriety. I noticed that showy tender caresses were allowed in public, and this did not appeal to me at all; in fact nothing could have been more painful, and I disliked it heartily.

One must resign oneself to the *incalculability* of the habits which women contract in the name of modesty. A common woman, by overdoing modesty, can believe she has become the equal of a fine lady.

The power of modesty is so great that a sensitive woman may betray her feelings to her lover rather by actions than by words.

The prettiest, richest, and easiest woman in Bologna has just confided to me that last night a little coxcomb of a Frenchman —an odd advertisement for his country that is staying here at the moment— took it into his head to hide under her bed. Apparently he was determined not to waste a great number of absurd declarations with which he has been plaguing her for a month. But the fine gentleman lacked presence of mind. He waited until Madame M. had dismissed her maid and retired to bed, but he was too impatient to allow time for people to fall asleep. She sprang for the bell and had him ignominiously thrown out, with half a dozen footmen shouting at him and beating him.

"And suppose he had waited a couple of hours?" I asked her.

"Ah, then I should have been in a sorry plight," she replied; "everyone will believe," he would have said, 'I came here because you asked me to.'"[49]

After leaving my pretty friend, I called to see a woman more worthy of love than any other I know. Her extreme delicacy of feeling exceeds, if that be possible, her touching beauty. I found her alone, and told her the story of Madame M. We discussed it.

"Just a moment," she said, "if this woman already liked the man who chose to do such a thing, she would forgive him, and later on fall in love with him."

I must admit that I was stunned at the unexpected light this threw upon the depths of the human heart. After a pause, I said:

"But when a man is in love, is he brave enough to resort to violent extremes of that kind?"

This chapter would have been a good deal more to the point if it had been written by a woman. Only on hearsay evidence can I offer any comment on matters relating to feminine pride and vanity, the habit of modesty carried to excess, and certain *refinements of feeling* exclusive to women, which depend solely on interrelated sensations,[50] and often have no natural basis.

In a moment of philosophical frankness a woman once told me something like tins:

"If I were ever to give up my liberty, the man I should ultimately choose would set a higher value on my feelings because I had always been sparing of even the lightest preference before." A charming woman may thus treat a man now with extreme coldness, because she is saving herself for a future lover whom she may never even meet. This is the prime excess of modesty; the second comes from women's vanity; and the third from the vanity of their husbands.

It seems to me that this potential love is often present in

the most virtuous women's daydreams, and rightly so. When heaven has endowed you with a soul made for love, not to love is to deny yourself and others of great happiness. It is as if an orange-tree dared not flower for fear of committing a sin. And remember that a soul made for love can never be satisfied with any other kind of happiness. After its first taste of the much-vaunted pleasures of the world, it finds them intolerably dull, and though it often believes itself fond of Art and the sublimities of nature, these merely lead the soul back to love, and more intensely than before, if that be possible. The soul soon realizes that it is being reminded of a happiness it has forsworn.

What I have against modesty is that it encourages untruthfulness; only in this respect have loose women the advantage of sensitive ones. A woman of easy virtue can say: "My dear, as soon as you please me I'll tell you, and I shall be as happy as you about it, for I have a great respect for you."

Look at the keen satisfaction of *Constance* after her lover's victory, when she exclaimed: "Oh, how glad I am that I have never given myself to anyone in the eight years since I quarreled with my husband." However absurd the reasoning in this, its joy strikes me as thoroughly refreshing.

I really must tell you here about the regrets of a certain lady of Seville, jilted by her lover. I must ask you to remember that in love everything is meaningful. Above all, please make allowances for my style.

With a man's eyes, I can see nine characteristics of *modesty*.

1. A woman is staking much against little. So, her extreme reserve and often affectation; she does not, for instance, laugh at the things which are in fact the most amusing. Hence, also, her need for a high degree of intelligence if she is to achieve just the right degree of modesty.[51] Many women fall short in this respect at small informal gatherings, or rather they do not insist enough that the stories they hear are at first decently veiled, and become more explicit only as the party becomes more bacchanalian.[52]

Is it a result of modesty and its deadly tedium for some women that most of them seem to admire men's brashness more than anything else? Or do they perhaps mistake brashness for character?

2. Second law: My lover will respect me the more for it.

3. Force of habit controls modesty even at the most passionate moments.

4. Modesty both pleases and flatters a lover, stressing

the laws which are being transgressed for his sake.

5. Modesty must make women's pleasures more *intoxicating:* the stronger the habit these pleasures have to overcome, the greater the turmoil they produce. If the Comte de Valmont finds himself in a pretty woman's bedroom at midnight, why, that happens to him every week, but to her perhaps only once in two years. Rarity and modesty combined in this way must offer women infinitely keener pleasures.[53]

6. The one drawback of modesty is that it inevitably leads to untruthfulness.

7. Modesty carried to excess is harsh, discouraging the sensitive and shy from loving. Meaning the ones, in fact, who were made for the purpose of giving and enjoying the delights of love.

8. If a sensitive woman has had but few lovers, modesty is an impediment to ease of behavior, and she runs the risk of being led to some extent by friends who are not so impeded. Instead of relying on blind habit, she studies each situation on its merits, and her delicate modesty lends a little constraint to all her actions. In fact, by behaving naturally she appears artificial and awkward, but it is awkwardness more like the grace of heaven.

If the friendliness of such women sometimes seems like tenderness, it is because, though angels, they are flirts without knowing it.

Reluctant to interrupt their reverie or to take the trouble of finding something pleasant and polite, just polite, to say to a friend, they will lean tenderly upon his arm.[1]

9. When women become writers they rarely achieve sublimity. Yet, the little notes they write are delightful, because they are never more than half way to frankness. For women frankness is like going out undressed. A man generally writes entirely under the spell of his imagination, and without knowledge of what he is driving at.

Summing Up

It is a common mistake to behave towards women as if they were a more generous and emotional kind than men, and against whom it is not necessary to compete. It is too easily forgotten that in addition to the normal bent of humanity, there are two particular and peculiar laws which dominate these creatures of emotion; I mean: feminine pride, and modesty, with the often unaccountable habits born of modesty.

Chapter 27 — About *Glances*

Glances are the big guns of the virtuous flirt; everything can be conveyed in a look, and yet that look can always be denied, because it cannot be quoted word for word.

It reminds me of Comte Giraud, the Mirabeau of Rome.

Because of the nice little Government of this part of the world he has developed a singular method of communication, using amputated words which mean everything and yet nothing. By conveying his meaning widely, you cannot compromise him, however much you quote him verbatim. Cardinal Lante accused him of having stolen this method from women. And I would say that even the most honest woman knows the trick. It is a cruel but just retaliation for man's tyranny.

Chapter 28 — About *Feminine Pride*

All their lives women hear men talk about things that are supposed to be important: success in finance and in war, deaths in duels, shocking or well-deserved vengeance, and so forth.

Realizing that they —spirited women— cannot hope to be proud in these important fields, they let such matters alone. They know that in their bosoms beat hearts whose emotions are stronger and loftier than their surroundings, yet they see that even the meanest of men are accorded more respect than themselves. They see that they themselves can only be proud in little things, or at least in things whose importance is only measurable in terms of feelings, and which an outsider cannot judge.

Tortured by the painful contrast between the pettiness

of their lot and the loftiness of their spirit, women decide that their pride shall be respected by the very vehemence of its manifestation or by the implacable tenacity with which they uphold their exclusions. Women of this sort, before intimacy, think themselves fortresses besieged by their lovers. They are irritated by the latters' advances, though these are only marks of love, and the lovers *are,* after all, in love. Yet instead of enjoying the expressions of their lovers' cares, women grow conceited, and when they do fall in love, however sensitive they may have been before, they have nothing left but vanity.

A generous woman would lay down her life a thousand times for her lover, yet would break with him forever on a trivial point of pride as to whether a door should be left open or shut. It is a matter of honor. Even Napoleon fell because he would not abandon a village.

I have known a quarrel of this kind last longer than a year. A very wonderful woman was throwing away all her happiness rather than let her lover entertain the smallest doubt about her overweening pride. They became reconciled quite by chance and because the woman was unable to master a moment of weakness. At a time when she thought he was a hundred miles away, she met her lover in a place where he was certainly not expecting to see *her.* She could not conceal her first impulse of joy, and the man was even more moved than she was. They almost fell into each other's arms, and I have never seen such floods of tears; it was the unexpected vision of happiness, and tears are the ultimate smile.

The Duke of Argyll showed great presence of mind in avoiding a conflict with feminine pride during his interview at Richmond with Queen Caroline.[54] The nobler the character of a woman is, the more dreadful are these storms:

... As the blackest sky
Foretells the heaviest tempest.

Don Juan

Perhaps the greater a woman's day-to-day delight in the distinguished qualities of her lover, the more she seeks revenge, in those moments of cruelty when sympathy seems inverted, for seeing him usually as better than other people. She is afraid she may be grouped with the others.

It's been a long time since I read that boring book *Clarissa Harlowe;* I seem to remember, though, that it was feminine pride which made her pine to death rather than accept the hand of Lovelace.

Lovelace was gravely at fault; but since she was a little in love with him she should have found it in her heart to forgive a crime committed in love's name.

Monime, on the other hand, strikes me as a tender

symbol of feminine delicacy. To hear an actress worthy of the part recite these lines must bring a flush of pleasure to all but a few:

Et ce fatal amour, don't j'avais triomphe,

Vos detours l'ont surpris et m'en ont convaincue,

Je vous l'ai confesse, je le dois soutenir;

En vain vous en pourriez perdre le souvenir;

Et cet aveu honteux, ou vous m'avez forcee,

Demeurera toujours present a ma pensee.

Toujours je vous croirais incertain de ma foi;

Et le tombeau, seigneur, est moins triste pour moi

Que le lit d'un epoux qui m'a fait cet outrage;

Et, qui, me preparant un eternel ennui,

M'a fait rougir d'un feu qui n'etait pas pour lui.

Racine.

I can see future generations finding here a justification of monarchy[55] having produced characters of this sort and their images in great art.

However, even in the medieval republics, I can find an excellent example of this delicacy which seems to oppose my theory of the influence of governments upon passions; but in all fairness I must include it. I refer to these moving lines by Dante:

Deh! quando tu sarai tomato al mondo,

Ricorditi di me,che son la Pia:

Siena mi fe': disfecemi Maremma;

Salsi colui, che innanellata pria,

Disposando, m'avea con la sua gemma.

Purgatorio, C.V.[56]

The woman who speaks here with so much control had suffered in secret the fate of Desdemona, and could by a word have revealed her husband's crime to her friends still on earth.

Nello della Pietra married Madonna Pia, sole heiress of the Tolomei family, the richest and noblest in Siena. Her beauty was the envy of all Tuscany, and her husband became excessively jealous of her. His jealousy, poisoned by a false report and ever-recurrent suspicion, led him to plan a wicked crime. Although it is difficult to conclude today whether his wife was entirely innocent, certainly Dante would have us think so.

Her husband took her to the Maremma, the marshy salt flats near Siena, which were then, as now, notorious for the effects of their *aria cattiva* (noxious vapors). He would never explain to his unfortunate wife why she was exiled in so dangerous a place; his pride never condescended to complaint or accusation. He lived alone with her in a solitary tower, whose ruins I have visited by the sea-shore; maintaining a disdainful silence, and refusing to answer the questions of his young wife, or even to listen to her prayers.

Coldly he waited for the pestilential atmosphere to take effect, and it was not long before the miasma of the marshes began to play havoc with those features reputed to be the loveliest of the century. Before many months had passed she was dead. Some chroniclers of those far-off days suggest that Nello used a dagger to hasten her departure, but even her contemporaries were uncertain about the manner of her death beyond that she died horribly, out in the marshlands.

Nello della Pietra lived on and passed the rest of his days in unbroken silence.

Nothing could be nobler and more gentle than the way the young Pia speaks to Dante, asking to be remembered to the friends on earth she had left behind so early; but in speaking of herself and her husband she makes not the least complaint of unspeakable and irreparable cruelty, only suggesting that her husband knows the truth about her death.

I think it is only in Mediterranean countries that pride is so steadfast in its vengefulness.

In Piedmont I once was the involuntary witness of a similar case, but at the time I didn't know the full story. I had been dispatched with a force of twenty-five dragoons into the woods along the banks of the Sesia to prevent smuggling. Reaching this wild and lonely area towards evening, I saw through the trees the ruins of an old castle. As I moved nearer I found to my surprise that it was occupied. A local nobleman lived there, a sinister-faced fellow, forty years old and six feet tall. With a very bad grace he gave me two rooms, where I used to play music with my quartermaster. After some days we discovered that our host had a woman there whom we jokingly nicknamed Camille; but we had no suspicion of the horrible truth. Six weeks later, she died. A morbid desire urged me to see her in her coffin, and bribed a monk who was watching over her to admit me to the chapel in the middle of the night, on the pretext of sprinkling holy water. She had one of those superb faces that are lovely even in death, with a thin aquiline nose whose noble and tender contour I shall never forget. I left that gloomy spot soon afterwards. Five years later, when a detachment of my regiment was escorting the Emperor to his coronation as King of Italy, I had the whole story related to me. I learned that Count ____ the jealous husband, had one morning found, hooked upon his wife's bed, an English watch, the property of a young man who lived in their little town. That very day, he took her to the ruined castle in the Sesia woods. Like Nello della Pietra, he never spoke a word. When she begged him for some favor, he would coldly and silently show her the English watch, which he always carried with him. In this way he lived alone with her for almost three years. In the end she died of despair, while still in the full bloom of life. Her husband tried to knife the owner of the watch, failed, took ship from Genoa and has never been heard of since. His estate has been divided up.

When in the presence of women with feminine pride, you must accept insults gracefully—an easy matter for anyone accustomed to army life—the proud beauties are irked. They take you for a weakling, and soon begin to insult you themselves. These haughty characters practically throw themselves into the arms of men who are totally intolerant of others. This is, I think, the only line to take, so that you often have to pick a quarrel with your neighbor to avoid one with your mistress.

Miss Cornel, the celebrated London actress, once saw her rich and extremely useful colonel entering her rooms unexpectedly, where she was entertaining some little nonentity of a lover who was just pleasant company. In a trembling voice she introduced him to the colonel:

"Mr So-and-so has called to look at that pony I want to sell."

"I have called for no such thing!" exclaimed the little man. She had been bored with him, but from the moment he made this spunky rejoinder she began to love him all over again.[57] Such women share in their lovers' pride, rather than pitting their own spirited dispositions against it.

The personality of the Duke of Lauzun —the 1660 duke, that is[58]— would have appealed to women of this kind, if they could initially excuse his lack of social graces. The finer points of greatness elude them, mistaking for coldness the cool gaze which sees everything unperturbed by petty details. I have even heard the court ladies at Saint-Cloud maintaining that Napoleon was pretty dry and prosaic.[59]

A great man is like an eagle; the higher he soarss the less you can see of him, and loneliness is the price he pays for being great.

Feminine pride causes what women call *breaches of delicacy*. I think these are not unlike what kings call *lese-majeste*, a crime all the more risky since it may be committed quite unsuspectingly. Lacking sparkle, the most ardent lover may be accused of offending delicacy, or — sadder still— if he dares to treat himself to love's greatest delight: that happy state of being perfectly at ease with the beloved and oblivious to what is said to him.

These are the details that no gentleman would ever dream of suspecting. You must have suffered it to believe it, because you are so used to dealing fairly and squarely with your friends of the male sex.

Never forget that you are dealing with creatures who

think themselves, however mistakenly, your inferiors in strength of character, or rather, may think that you so regard them.

A woman's pride should really be founded on the strength of the feelings she can inspire. The wife of Francois I had a lady-in-waiting, who was forever being teased about the fickleness of her lover, of whom it was said that he hardly cared for her at all. A little later he fell ill, and when he reappeared at court was quite dumb. A couple of years after this, someone expressed surprise that she should still be in love with him; turning to her lover she said: "Speak!" And he spoke.

Chapter 29 — About *Women's Courage*

I tell thee, proud templar, that not in thy fiercest battles hadst thou displayed more of thy vaunted courage, than has been shewn by woman when called upon to suffer by affection or duty.
Ivanhoe. Vol. 3.

I recall coming across the following sentence in a history book: "All the men lost their heads; at moments like this women are incontestably their superiors."

Women's courage has a greater *reserve* than that of men. In a dangerous situation their self-respect is piqued, pitting themselves with pleasure against the men who have often wounded them with patronizing protectiveness and strength, that the momentum of this pleasure carries them over whatever fear weakens men at such a time.

Likewise, if a man were thus helped, would overcome all odds, for the fear is never part of the danger; it is within us.

Not that I am trying to minimize women's courage. I have at times seen women braver than the bravest men. Only they must have a man to be in love with, for then they feel only through him, reacting to direct and personal danger of the most deadly kind as if it were a flower to be plucked in his presence.[60]

I have also seen women who are not in love display the coolest and most unexpected fearlessness and nerve, thinking at the time, though, that they were only brave because they did not know how beastly a wound could be.

As for moral courage, which greatly exceeds the other kind, the resolve of a woman who will not surrender to her lover is beyond all admiration. Any other mark of courage is a mere trifle by comparison with so painful and unnatural a struggle. Perhaps they find strength in the habit of sacrifice which modesty compels.

One of the misfortunes of women is that the proof of this moral courage must always remain secret, and is almost incommunicable.

A still greater misfortune is that this courage must

always be used against their own happiness; the Princesse de Cleves should have said nothing to her husband and yielded to M. de Nemours.

Perhaps women are sustained mainly by their pride in a well-conducted defense, imagining that their lovers in order to win them are seeking to satisfy a point of vanity. A mean and petty idea, this, that a passionate man should plunge from lightheadedness into a series of situations where he makes a fool of himself, and yet have time to think about points of vanity! It's like the monks who think they are cheating the devil, and reward themselves by taking a pride in their hair shirts and mortifications of the flesh.

If Madame de Cleves had reached the ripe old age when one looks back on life and sees how empty were the pleasures of pride, she would have repented. She would have preferred to have lived like Madame de la Fayette.[61]

Having just re-read a hundred pages of this essay, I seem to have given a remarkably poor idea of true love, the love which pervades the whole consciousness and fills it with pictures, some wildly happy, some hopeless—yet all sublime.

True love blinds one to everything else in the world.

I am at a loss to express what I can see so clearly; I have never been so painfully aware of my lack of talent. In what intelligible terms can I express the simplicity of gesture and bearing, the deep earnestness, the look that bears the precise nuance of feeling so exactly and so candidly, and above all, I repeat, the ineffable unconcern about everything but the woman one loves.

A *yes* or a *no* spoken by a man in love has a *warmth* and *grace* not to be found elsewhere, nor even in the same man at other times.

This morning (3rd August) at about nine o'clock I rode past the Marquis of Zampieri's English garden, which lies on the last slopes of the heavily-wooded hills which back Bologna, overlooking a magnificent view of Lombardy, rich and green, the most beautiful countryside in the world. As I passed Zampieri's garden, on my way to the falls of the Reno at Casa-Lecchio, in a laurel glade which overlooked the road I saw Count Delfante, in profound reverie, and although we had spent the previous evening together until two o'clock in the morning, he barely answered my salutation.

Approaching the falls, I crossed the Reno. At least three hours later, on my way back, I saw him again, still in Zampieri's laurel glade, exactly as he had been before, leaning against a tall pine which soared above the laurels. I am afraid the reader may find this anecdote too simple, proving nothing; but Delfante came up to me, tears in his eyes, and begged me not to tell the story of his immobility.

I was touched and suggested we went back together the way I had just come, to spend the rest of the day in the country. Two hours later he had told me everything; his was a fine soul, and the pages you have just read are cold by comparison with what he told me!

In the second place, he thought his love was *not returned;* here I disagree with him. The lovely marble face of Countess Ghigi, with whom he had passed the evening, is quite inscrutable, yet once in a while a sudden little blush which she cannot control betrays the feelings of a soul torn between strong emotion and the most exalted feminine pride. The blush tinges her alabaster neck, and what can be glimpsed of those lovely shoulders worthy of Canova. She is expert at deflecting her dark eyes from the penetrating scrutiny of those whom her feminine delicacy fears to encounter; but last night I saw her blush all over when Delfante said something to which she took exception. Her proud soul found him the less worthy of her because of it.

But when all is said and done, even if I am mistaken about Delfante's good fortune, I think he is happier than me since I am indifferent, although in appearance and reality I am in a very fortunate condition.

Bologna, 3rd August 1818

Women with their feminine pride, take revenge on intelligent men for having to suffer fools, and upon generous hearts for the dullness of wealthy, insolent bores. Let's admit that this is a pretty sorry state of affairs.

Some women are made unhappy by petty details of pride and social convention, and have been placed in an intolerable position by the pride of their relatives. In generous recompense for all their misfortunes, Destiny decreed that they should know the bliss of loving and being loved with passion.

But there comes a day when they borrow from their enemies that same insane pride which had made them unhappy, only to destroy the unique happiness left to them, and to bring misfortune upon themselves and those who love them. Some women friend, who may have had a dozen affairs, perhaps more than one at a time, will persuade them gravely that if they fall in love they will be dishonored in the eyes of the public. And yet this noble public, whose aspirations never rise above the most base, generously credits all women with a new lover each year because, says the public, "that is the way things usually happen!"

Hence the saddening and odd spectacle of a tender and supremely fastidious woman, and angel of purity, fleeing on the advice of some corrupt fool from the one matchless happiness within her reach, run to appear radiantly dressed in white, before some great lout of a judge, notoriously blind these hundred years, who shouts at the top of his voice: "She is wearing black!"

Chapter 31 — Extract from Salviati's Diary

Ingenium nobis ipsa puella facit.[Wit makes the lady]
Propertius, 2. I.

Bologna, 29th April, 1818

Love has reduced me to misery and despair, and I curse my very existence. I can take no interest in anything. The weather is gloomy and wet, and a late cold spell has plunged all nature back into sadness just when, after a long winter, everything was thrusting towards spring.

Schiassetti, a colonel on half-pay, a cool, rational friend, came and spent two hours with me.

"You ought to give up loving her."

"But how can I? Can you give me back my enthusiasm for soldiering?"

"It's a great pity you ever met her."

I almost agreed with him, feeling dejected and low-spirited; so much has melancholy taken possession of me. Together we mused about what her friend had to gain by speaking ill of me to her, and we could find no answer but the Neapolitan proverb: "When youth and love leave a woman she takes offence at anything." One thing is certain, anyway: this woman friend is morbidly against me; the word was used by a friend of hers. I could get my revenge in the most beastly way, but I haven't the slightest defense against her hatred.

Schiassetti left, and I went out into the rain wondering what would become of me. My lodgings, this sitting-room where I lived during the first days of our acquaintance when I used to see her every day, have now become insufferable. Every print on the wall, every stick of furniture, reproaches me for the happiness I dreamed of in this room, and which is now lost forever.

Striding through the streets under a cold rain; chance, if you can call it chance, led me past her windows. Night was falling, and as I walked by, my tear-filled eyes fixed upon the window of her room.

Suddenly the curtain was lifted for a second, as if for a glimpse of the square outside, and then it quickly fell back into place.

Feeling a spasm in my heart, I could no longer hold myself up, and took refuge in a neighboring portico. My feelings were running riot; it might of course have been a chance movement of the curtain; but suppose it had been her hand that lifted it!

There are only two miseries in life: the misery of unrequited passion, and that of the dead blank.

In love, I have the feeling that boundless happiness beyond my wildest dreams is just round the corner, waiting only for a word or a smile.

Without a passion like Schiassetti's, through dull days, I can find no happiness anywhere, and I begin to doubt whether it is in store for me at all. I am turning sour. It would be better not to have strong passions and to be only a little curious or vain.

It is now two o'clock in the morning, and I saw her curtain move at six last night. I have paid ten calls and been to the theatre, but I was silent and moody everywhere, and spent the evening brooding over this question: "After being so angry, and with so little cause —for after all, did I mean to give offence, and what is there in this world that a good intention cannot palliate?— after her anger, did she feel a moment of love?"

Poor Salviati, who wrote these words in his copy of Petrarch, died a short time afterwards. He was a close friend of mine and of Schiassetti's, and were privy to all his thoughts, and I have drawn upon him for the more depressing side of this essay. He was imprudence personified, and the woman for whom he did so many foolish things is the most interesting person I have ever encountered. Schiassetti used to tell me that Salviati's unhappy passion had really been a blessing in disguise. For in the first place Salviati had just suffered a severe financial setback, which compelled him to live very modestly, though his youth had been dazzling. In any other circumstances he would have been beside himself with anger at his misfortune, but as it was he didn't think of it once in a fortnight.

Secondly, and this too was important in another way given the kind of mind he had, his passion was the first real course in logic he had ever taken. That may seem odd in a man who had been at court, but the answer lies in the man's supreme courage. For instance he never flinched that day in 18__ when all his hopes were shattered. He was surprised, as he had been before in Russia, that he did not feel anything out of the ordinary, and it is a fact that he has never been sufficiently afraid of anything to think about it for two consecutive days. Instead of being inattentive he now sought every moment to have courage; till now he had never been aware of danger.

When, as a result of his imprudence and of his faith that people would not misconstrue things,[62] Salviati was condemned to see only twice a month the woman he loved, we occasionally saw him mad with joy, praising her the whole night through, because she had received him with that noble candor for which he adored her. He maintained that he and Mme — were two souls quite outside the common run, who could understand each other at a glance. He could not grasp that she might pay the least attention to parochial, small-minded misconstructions which could make him appear criminal. His reward for this generous faith in a woman surrounded by his enemies was to have the door shut in his face.

"Where Mme — is concerned," I used to tell Salviati, "you forget your principles, and also that one should never believe in great-heartedness except as a last resort."

"Do you think," he replied, "there could be anyone else in the world whose heart is so much akin to hers as mine is? Admittedly I am paying for my particular kind of passion, which makes me see an angry Leonore in the skyline of rocks at Poligny, and the price is that all my projects in real life are dogged by misfortune, a misfortune caused by a lack of consistency and a rashness resulting from the strength of fleeting impressions."

This is verging on sheer madness.

For Salviati life was divided into fortnightly periods colored by the last audience he had been granted by his beloved. But I noticed more than once that the happiness he was given by a welcome apparently less frigid than usual was considerably less intense than his misery after a cold reception.[63] Also Mme ____ was not always frank with him, and these are the only two criticisms I have ever dared to offer him. Apart from his most intimate distress, which he always took care to withhold even from his dearest and least envious friends, he regarded a cold reception from Leonore as a victory of prosaic and calculating natures over frank and generous ones. At such times he lost his faith in virtue and even in glory, talking to his friends only about sorrowful ideas whose truth his passion led him to assert, but which did have some philosophical interest. I watched his peculiar personality with curiosity; passionate love is normally found only in rather simple, rather German people.[64] Salviati, on the other hand, had one of the soundest and keenest minds I have ever known.

I believe he was only happy, after these cold visits, when he had found some justification for Leonore's severities. If he felt that she had been in any way at fault in ill-treating him, this made him unhappy. I should never have believed that love could be so free from vanity.

He never tired of sounding love's praises:

"If some supernatural power said to me: 'Break this watch-glass and Leonore will revert to what she was three years ago — a mere acquaintance,' I do not believe that I should ever have the courage to break it."

So frantic he looked arguing this that I never dared to

draw his attention to the foregoing criticisms.

He added: "Just as Luther's Reformation shook society to its foundations at the end of the Middle Ages and thus renewed and rebuilt the world on a rational basis, so a generous person is renewed and restored by love.

"Only then does he put away all the childish things of life. Without love's upheaval he would always suffer in some way from heaviness or theatricality. It is only since I fell in love that I have learned how to be noble, because of our "military college" education is so hopeless.

"Although I behaved myself, I was a mere child at Napoleon's court and in Moscow. I did my duty, but I was unaware of the heroic simplicity which comes from entire and whole-hearted self-sacrifice. For instance, it is only within the last year that I have come to grasp the simplicity of Livy's Romans. Before, I found them dull by comparison with our own dashing colonels. What they did for their Rome, I find in my heart for Leonore. If I were fortunate enough to be allowed to do something for her, my first impulse would be to keep it a secret. The conduct of a Regulus or a Decius was something settled in advance, and so could give them no surprise. I was petty-minded, before I fell in love, precisely because I was at times tempted to consider myself great. I was conscious of the effort I was making and congratulated myself upon it.

"And in the sphere of the affections, love is all-important. After the chance experiences of early youth, one's heart closes up against sympathy. Death or distance alienates you from childhood friends, and you are thrown upon the company of associates quite indifferent to you, and who, foot-rule in hand, are forever calculating in terms of self-interest or vanity. Gradually all that is sensitive and generous withers from lack of nurture and before you reach thirty you have become callous to sweet or tender sensations. In the midst of this arid desert, love makes a spring burst forth, bursting with feelings sweeter and more abundant than those of early youth. Then there was hope, vague, crazy, and easily distracted;[65] there was no devotion to anything, no deep constant desires; youth, always fickle, craved for novelty, adoring one day what it neglected the next. But not one thing is more contemplative, more mysterious, more eternally single in its aim than love's crystallization. Once it was only pleasant things which had the right to please, and the pleasure they gave was no more than momentary; but now all that has any bearing on the woman one loves, even the most irrelevant object, moves one deeply. Once when I arrived in a large town a hundred miles from Leonore's home, I discovered that I was trembling with shyness, quaking at every street corner, afraid I should meet Alviza, her intimate friend whom I did not even know by sight. Everything seemed to have taken on a mysterious and sacred glow; my heart pounded as I spoke to an elderly scholar. If anyone mentioned the city gate near the house where Leonore's friend lives, I blushed scarlet.

"The very harshness of the beloved is infinite grace, which is not to be found in any other woman even at her best. In just the same way the great shadows in Correggio's pictures are unlike those of other painters. Usually shadows are necessary to give value to highlights and to throw faces into relief, and are otherwise not particularly pleasing; but Correggio's shadows have magical grace in their own right, enwrapping us in sweet reverie.[66]

"Yes, half of life, its most wonderful half, is hidden from the man who has never loved passionately."

It needed all Salviati's argumentative powers to stand up to the wisdom of Schiassetti, who time and again told him:

"If you want to be happy, be content with a life free from care and a little good fortune every day. Don't be drawn into the gamble of a grand passion."

And Salviati would reply: "Lend me a little of your curiosity, then."

Some days Salviati would have liked to follow the advice of our wise old colonel. He resisted a little and thought he was succeeding, but it was a quite unequal struggle in spite of all his superior force of character.

When far down the street, he saw a white satin hat that looked like the one Mme ____ wore, his heart skipped a beat, and he had to lean against the wall for support. Even in his saddest moments, the happiness of meeting her always left him intoxicated for some hours despite the effects of all his misfortunes and of every attempt to reason with him.[67]

In sum, it must be said that when he died,[68] after two years of this boundless and generous passion, his character had assumed nobility in several ways, and in this respect at least he had judged himself correctly. Had he lived, and if circumstances had helped him a little, he would have got himself talked of; though given its very simplicity, his merit would have passed unnoticed on this earth.

O *lasso!*
Quanti dolci pensier, quanto disio,
Meno costui *al doloroso passo!*
Biondo era e bello, e di gentile aspetto;
Ma l'un de' cigli un colpo avea diviso.[69]
Dante

Chapter 32 — About *Intimacy*

The greatest happiness love can offer is the first

pressure of hands between you and your beloved.

The particular pleasures of gallantry are, on the contrary, much more real and much more frequently the subject of witticisms.

In passionate love, intimacy is not so much the perfect happiness, but the last step on the way to it.

But how can we describe happiness, if it leaves no traces of memories?

Mortimer was returning from a long journey, in a state of agitation. He adored Jenny, but she had left his letters unanswered. No sooner was he back in London than he rode to her country house to find her. When he arrived, she was out walking in the grounds.

He ran to her, his heart pounding.

They met, and she gave him her hand and greeted him in some confusion; he saw that she loved him. Strolling along the paths, Jenny's dress caught upon a prickly acacia bush. Later Mortimer won his heart's desire, but Jenny was unfaithful to him. I maintain that she never loved him, but he says that the way she received him on his return from the Continent is proof enough of her love. Yet he cannot recall a single detail of their meeting. However, he is clearly shaken by the sight of an acacia, and this is really the only distinct memory he has preserved of the happiest moment in his life.[70]

A former knight, who is both sensitive and frank, told me about some of his love affairs this evening, as we crouched in the bottom of our boat in rough weather on Lake Garda.[71] I shall not betray his confidences to the public, but I think I may be allowed to draw from them the conclusion that the moment of intimacy is like those lovely days in May, a critical time for the finest flowers; a time which can be deadly and wither the brightest hopes in a moment.

Simplicity is extremely important. It is the only coquetry allowed in something as serious as a love like that of *Werther,* when all sense of direction is lost. At the same time, by a happy coincidence, it is the best tactic. With no malice, a man who is really in love says the most delightful things, and speaks in a language unknown to him.

Woe be to the man who shows even a trace of affectation!

Even when he is in love, even if he is a genius, he loses three quarters of his advantage. If you give way to affectation for a moment, you will be met with curtness a minute later.

The whole art of loving seems to me, in a nutshell, to consist in saying precisely what the degree of intoxication requires at any given moment. In other words, you must listen to your heart. You must not think this is easy; if you are truly in love and your lover says things which make you happy, you will lose the power of speech.

You are thus deprived of the actions to which your words would have led,[72] and it is better to stay silent than to say tender things at the wrong moment. What was apt ten seconds earlier does not remain so, and will be inept ten seconds later. Whenever I failed to obey this rule,[73] and said something that had come into my head three minutes before and which sounded pretty, Leonore was sure to punish me. Afterwards, as I left, I would say to myself: "She's right; that sort of thing must be thoroughly shocking for a well-bred woman, it's an indecency of feeling."

Like verbose talkers of indifferent taste, they would rather permit a certain weakness or coldness. Their only concern is lest their lover be false, so that the least insincerity in the smallest detail, no matter how innocent, quickly annuls their happiness, putting them on the defensive.

Honest women are averse to what is vigorous or unexpected, even though these are symptoms of passion; besides, vigor alarms modesty and women recoil from it.

After your blood has been cooled by some hint of jealousy or displeasure, you can well engage in the sort of conversation that promotes that intoxication in which love thrives, and if after the first two or three stages of the discussion you seize the opportunity to say exactly what comes into your mind, you will give your beloved keen satisfaction.

Most people make the mistake of trying to bring in some remark which they consider pretty, witty, or moving, instead of relaxing from traditional weightiness into a natural intimacy which allows them to say in simple terms whatever they feel at the time. If you have the courage to do this your reward will be in the nature of reconciliation.

This swift and unsolicited reward for the pleasure that you give your beloved is what raises love so high above the other passions.

If you are perfectly natural there will be a complete fusion of the happiness of both of you.[74] Because of fellowship and various other laws which govern our natures, this is, quite simply, the greatest happiness that can exist.

It is easy to define what we mean by *being natural:* that necessary condition for happiness in love.

We call an action *natural* when it does not differ from the habitual mode of action. It goes without saying that not only must you never tell a lie to your beloved, but you must refrain from the least embellishment of truth which could spoil its purity. For the act of embellishment occupies your attention, which can no longer respond unaffectedly, like the keys of a piano, to the feelings which show in her eyes.

She soon realizes it, through goodness knows what sense of coldness, and then she in turn falls back upon coquetry.

Isn't this the hidden reason why we find it impossible to love women whose intelligence is markedly inferior?

In their presence we can pretend with impunity, and since pretense is easier, from force of habit, we yield to the temptation *not* to be natural. From then on love is no longer love, but shrinks to one of the common affairs of life; the only difference is that instead of money we gain pleasure or self-satisfaction, or a mixture of both.

But it is difficult not to feel a shade of contempt for a woman whom you can hoodwink with impunity; consequently, she is thrown over as soon as a better-one appears on the scene. Habit or vows may hold things together; but I am talking about the inclination of the heart, which turns directly towards the greatest pleasure.

To come back to this word *natural:* to act naturally and to act habitually are two different things. If you take them as one and the same, then clearly the more sensitive you are the less easy it is to be natural, because your behavior is less dominated by habit and your whole personality is more to the front in your response to each situation.

Every next page in the life story of a man without

passion is the same as the previous one; take him today, take him yesterday, he is still the same block of wood.

A sensitive man, once his heart is stirred, loses all memory of habit as a guide to action; how can he keep on the track when he has lost the scent?

He is aware of the enormous weight attaching to every word he speaks to his beloved, and feels that a word may decide his fate, hardly avoiding to express himself well, nor help feeling that he *is* speaking well. From that moment candor is lost. There must, therefore, be no pretensions to candor, which is a mark of those who are not turned in upon themselves. We are what we succeed in being, but we are conscious of what we are.

We have now reached the last essence of natural behavior to which, in love, the most fastidious soul can claim.

As a last anchor against the storm, the passionate lover can only cling to a pledge to read his heart accurately and never to alter one jot of the truth. If the conversation is lively and often interrupted, he can expect several good spells of being natural; if not, he will succeed in being natural only when his love is at a little less than fever pitch.

In your beloved's presence even *physical movements* almost cease to be natural, although the habit of them is so deeply ingrained in the muscles. Whenever I gave my arm to Leonore, I always felt I was about to fall, and I had to think how to walk. The best that can be hoped for is never to show affectation deliberately; convince yourself that failure to be natural is the greatest possible danger to your interests and may easily lead to disaster. Your beloved's heart gets out of harmony with yours and you lose that sharp spontaneous interplay where frankness responds to frankness. This is to lose every means of moving her — I almost said of seducing her.

Not that I want to deny that a woman worthy of love can link her destiny with the pretty motto of the ivy:

"With nothing to cling to, I die."

The thing is a law of nature, but for a woman to make her lover happy is always a decisive step to take for her own happiness. A sensible woman is not going to concede everything to her lover until she can no longer defend herself. Now the slightest suspicion about her lover's sincerity immediately renews her strength, at least enough to put off surrender for another day.[75]

Need I add that to make all the foregoing utterly absurd, one has only to apply it to mannered love?

Chapter 33 — A little doubt

Always set a little doubt at rest, that's what keeps one craving, that's what keeps happy love alive. Because the

119

misgivings are always there, the pleasures never grow tedious. This kind of happiness is marked by extreme earnestness.

Chapter 34 — About *Confidences*

No indiscretion is more quickly punished than to tell an intimate friend about your passionate love affairs. Your friend knows that if what you say is true your pleasures are a thousand times greater than his, and that you will be contemptuous of his.

Among women these things are worse still, since their object in life is to inspire passion, and since the confidante, too, has usually displayed her own charms before the same lover's eyes.

Still, when you are in the grip of this fever, there can be no more compelling moral need than a friend to whom you can confide the fearsome doubts which constantly assail you, since in this terrible passion *whatever you imagine invariably comes to exist.*

Salviati wrote in 1817: "A major flaw in my character (and in this I differ from Napoleon) is that when we are discussing the pros and cons of a passion and something has been morally proved, I can never use this as a firm basis. In spite of myself, and indeed to my great discomfort, I keep calling it in question." It is easy enough to be brave where ambition is concerned. A crystallization not subject to the desire of the thing sought serves to strengthen courage, but in love it is enslaved by the very thing against which that courage is needed.

A woman risks finding a friend false or bored.

Imagine a princess of thirty-five,[76] bored and plagued by a call for action, intrigue, and so forth ..., dissatisfied with her lukewarm lover, yet unable to inspire another. Imagine her at a loss to employ her restlessness, and with no distractions other than occasional bursts of spitefulness. She can easily find herself a pleasant pastime and an aim in life by making a genuine passion miserable, if the passion is misguided enough to be felt for someone other than herself, while her own lover drowses beside her.

This is the only case in which *hatred* can produce happiness; it provides a task and something to work at.

At first, when word of it spreads in society, the pleasure of doing something and the *challenge* to succeed make the task attractive. Jealousy of the lady is disguised as hatred of the lover; how else is it possible bitterly to hate a man you have never met? All awareness of envy is carefully excluded, for this implies an admission of merit, and there are always flatterers at hand to curry favor with jokes made at the expense of a good friend.

When the treacherous confidante behaves so wickedly,

she may well believe her only motive is to avoid losing a friendship she values. A woman who is bored will tell herself that even friendship can languish in a heart devoured by love and its mortal anxieties, and that such a friendship can only compete with love by confiding. Now, what could be more hateful to an envious woman than confidences of that kind?

The only confidences likely to be well received between women are those frankly delivered in the following vein: "My dear, there is an absurd and ruthless war waged against us by the prejudices customary among our tyrants. You help me today, and I'll do the same for you tomorrow."[77]

There is also the earlier exception when true friendship has survived from childhood days and has not since been spoilt by jealousy...

Confidences about passionate love are only well received between schoolboys in love with love, and between girls eaten up by curiosity, by tenderness seeking an outlet — perhaps already drawn by the instinct[78] which tells them this is the crucial business of their lives, and the sooner begun the better.

Everyone must have seen little girls of three very creditably discharging the obligations of gallantry.

Mannered love is stimulated by confidences, while

passionate love is cooled by them.

Confidences contain difficulties as well as dangers. In passionate love, what you cannot express (because language is too coarse to achieve the required nuance) exists none the less, only it is so fine drawn that error in observing it is more probable.

So, ad an observer under the stress of emotion observes badly, failing to give chance her due.

Possibly the wisest thing is to confide in oneself. Using borrowed names, but including all the relevant details, write down tonight what took place between you and your mistress, and the problems you are faced with. In a week's time, if you are suffering from passionate love, you will be someone else entirely, and then, on reading your case-history, you will be able to give yourself good advice.

Among men, whenever more than two are gathered together and envy might be aroused, politeness demands that the talk should be confined to physical love. The after-dinner conversation at men's parties is a case in point. Baffo's sonnets[79] are the ones recited, giving great pleasure because each person takes his neighbor's praise and enthusiasm literally, though very often the neighbor only wishes to appear gay or polite. French madrigals or the tender charm of Petrarch would be out of place.

When you are in love, no matter what you see or remember, whether you are packed in a gallery listening to political speeches, or riding at full gallop under enemy fire to relieve a garrison, you are always adding new perfections to your idea of your mistress, or finding new and ideal ways of making her love you more.

Each step your imagination takes brings a new delight. Little wonder that this state of mind is enticing.

Though the same habit persists, the moment you become jealous it produces an opposite effect. Far from giving you sublime joy each perfection added to the crown of your beloved, who perhaps loves another, is a dagger thrust in your heart. "This delight," cries a voice, "is for your rival!"[80]

And when other things strike you, instead of suggesting new ways of increasing her love, they say more of your opponent's advantages.

You see a pretty woman galloping in the park,[81] and the rival is promptly praised for his fine horses which can take him ten miles in fifty minutes.

This mood can easily turn to fury. You forget that in love *possession is nothing, only enjoyment matters.*

You overrate your competitor's success, and the insolence resulting from it. Then you reach the final torment: utter despair poisoning you even further by a shred of hope.

The only viable solution is to observe your rival's good fortune very closely. Often you will find him placidly dozing in the very drawing-room which contains the woman the thought of whom stops your heart beating when you see, far down a street, a hat which might be hers.

If you want him to wake up, just betray your jealousy. You will then perhaps have the privilege of informing him how valuable is this woman who prefers him to you, and you will be the author of his love for her.

As far as your rival is concerned there is no middle course; you must either joke with him in the most detached way, or frighten him off.

Since jealousy is the gravest of all ills, you can find an amusing diversion in risking your life. Because then your thoughts will not be entirely embittered (by the process described above) and you will be able to play with the idea of killing your rival.

Following the principle that one should never reinforce the strength of the enemy, you must conceal your love from your rival. Secretly, calmly, and simply, and on some pretext totally unrelated to love, you should say:

"Sir, I do not know why the public chooses to credit me with little Miss So-and-so, and is even so good as to believe me in love with her. If you wanted her, why, you could have her with all my heart, were it not that unfortunately I should be made to look a fool. In six months' time you can have all you want of her, but today the honor —heaven knows why attaches to these things— compels me to warn you, to my great regret, that if by any chance you unfairly do not await your turn, one of us will have to die."

Most probably your rival is not a passionate man, and may even be a very prudent one. Once he is convinced of your resolve he will readily surrender the woman upon the first convenient pretext. This is why your declaration must be made lightheartedly and the whole affair shrouded in the utmost secrecy.

What makes jealousy so painful is that you cannot employ vanity to help you bear it, but the method I have explained gives vanity a clear field. You may admire your own bravery, even if you are inclined to despise yourself as an inspirer of love.

If you would rather not be melodramatic, the best thing to do is to travel forty leagues and find a dancer to entertain, whose charms should appear to have halted you as you were passing.

Unless your rival has great insight, he will think you have[82] got over your passion.

Very often the best plan is to wait impassively until

your rival, by his own bungles, wears out his welcome with your beloved. Because, barring the case of a grand passion built up stage by stage in early youth, a woman will *not* love a fool for long.

In the case of jealousy after intimacy, you need both apparent indifference and genuine inconstancy, for many women, merely angry with a man they still love, will attach themselves to a man of whom their lover shows jealousy, until suddenly the game becomes a reality.[83]

I have treated this point in some detail because in these moments of jealousy one usually loses one's head, and advice written beforehand is a help. Besides, since the important thing is to pretend to keep calm, it is right and proper to learn the right atmosphere from philosophical writings.

Since you are only vulnerable by extending or denying things whose whole value depends on your passion, by managing fake indifference you disarm your adversaries with one blow.

If there is no action that can be taken, and you can amuse yourself by seeking solace, you will get some pleasure from reading *Othello*. Even the most damning appearances will be laid open to doubt, and you will pause delightedly over the words:

Trifles light as air

Seem to the jealous, confirmations strong

As proofs from holy writ.

Othello. Act III

I have even found consolation in a beautiful view of the sea:

The morning which had arisen calm and bright, gave a pleasant effect to the waste mountain view which was seen from the castle on looking to the landward; and the glorious Ocean crisped with a thousand rippling waves of silver, extended on the other side in awful yet complacent majesty to the verge of the horizon. With such scenes of calm sublimity, the human heart sympathizes even in HIS *most disturbed moods, and deeds of honor and virtue are inspired by their majestic influence.*

(The Bride of Lammermoor. **Vol. I.)**

In one of Salviati's manuscripts I found this:

"20th July, 1818. - A little unreasonably, I think, I often apply to life as a whole a feeling comparable to that of an ambitious man or of a good patriot during a battle, when he is tasked to look after reserve stores or ordered to some post away from danger and action. I should have been sorry to reach forty and to be past the age of loving, without having experienced passion deeply. I should have felt the bitter and degrading pain of realizing too late that I had been tricked into letting life go by without living.

"I spent three hours yesterday with the woman I love, in the presence of a rival whom she wishes me to believe is receiving her favors. There were admittedly bitter moments when I saw her lovely eyes gazing on him, and as I left I felt keen pangs of misery and despair. But what a host of new things! What vivid thoughts, and swift arguments! In spite of my rival's apparent good fortune, I felt with a rush of pride and delight that my love was far greater than his, telling myself that those cheeks would grow pale with fear at even the least of the sacrifices my love would joyfully make. For instance, I would gladly plunge my hand into a hat to take out one of two tickets: *'Be loved by her'* or *'Die at once'* and this feeling is so well established that I was able to make myself agreeable and take part in the conversation.

'If anyone had told me all this two years ago I should have laughed derisively.'

In the account of the voyage made by Captains Lewis and Clarke in 1806 to the sources of the River Missouri, I read this on page 215:

"Though poor, the *Ricaras* are kind and generous, and we stayed some time in three of their villages. Their women are the most beautiful of any tribe we have encountered. Moreover they are disinclined to keep their lovers in suspense. We found a further proof of the saying that to see the world is to discover that nothing is immutable. Among the *Ricaras,* it is a great breach of good behavior for a woman to grant her favors without the consent of her husband or brother. But, on the other hand, the husbands and brothers are delighted to be able to offer this little courtesy to their friends.

"There was a negro in our party who made a great impression on a people who had never seen a man of that color before. He was soon the favorite of the fair sex, and we observed that, far from displaying jealousy, the husbands were delighted when he visited their homes. The whole situation was enlivened by the fact that in such ramshackle huts as theirs everything was open to view."[84]

As for the woman you suspect to be disloyal, she is drifting apart from you because you have not stimulated crystallization and perhaps keep your place in her heart merely from habit. She is leaving you because she is too sure of you. You have removed fear, and the little doubts of happy love no longer occur; make her anxious, and above all beware of pointless protestations.

In the length of time you have known her you will no doubt have learned which woman in the town or in society she fears and envies most. Pay your attentions to this woman, but do not broadcast the fact. On the contrary, try to conceal it as hard as you can, putting your trust in the eyes of hatred to see all and realize all. The profound distaste you will feel for all women[85] for several months should make this easy for you. Remember that, placed as you are, you will spoil everything by showing your passion. So, see your beloved but seldom and drink champagne in convivial company.

In judging the quality of your mistress's love, remember that:

1. The more physical pleasure plays a basic part in love and in what in the beginning brought about intimacy, the more liable that love is to disloyalty and, still more, to unfaithfulness. This applies particularly to cases where the crystallization has been aided by the fires of youth at sixteen.

2. The loves of two people in love with each other are seldom the same.[86] Passionate love has its phases, when first one partner and then the other will be more in love. Often passionate love is answered with mere gallantry or vanity-love, and in general it is the woman who loves to distraction. Whatever kind of love one lover feels, no sooner is jealousy aroused than the other lover is required to fulfill all the conditions of passionate love.

Vanity produces all the needs of a tender heart in the jealous lover.

As a matter of fact nothing fatigues mannered love so

much as passionate love in the partner.

Quite often an intelligent man courting a woman merely turns her thoughts to love and melts her heart. She welcomes a man who is clever and pleases her, and he begins to entertain hopes.

One fine day this woman meets a man who makes her feel exactly what the clever man had described.

I have no idea what effect a man's jealousy has on the woman he loves. If she is bored with her lover, his jealousy must inspire thorough disgust, which may turn to hatred if the lover is less pleasant than the man of whom he is jealous, for according to Mme de Coulanges we only want jealousy in people of whom we ourselves could be jealous.

If she loves a man who is jealous without the right to be so, a woman's feminine pride —so difficult to recognize and respect— may be shocked. Spirited women, on the other hand, may be pleased by jealousy, as a new way of showing them their power.

Jealousy may be pleasant as a new way of proving love; or it may offend the modesty of an over-refined woman.

It may please by unveiling the mettle of the lover. Note that it is hot blood which is attractive and not bravery like Turenne's, which may well go with a cold heart.

It follows from the principle of crystallization that a woman should never say *yes* to a lover she has deceived if she wishes to make anything of him.

So great is the pleasure of continuing to enjoy our perfected image of the beloved that, until this fatal *yes,*

L'on va chercher bien loin, plutot que de mourir,

Quelque pretexte ami pour vivre et pour souffrir.

—Andre Chenier.

The story of Mademoiselle de Sommery is well known in France; how, surprised *in flagrante* by her lover, she boldly denied the whole thing. When he pressed her, she cried:

"Oh! I see it all now. You don't love me anymore; you'd rather believe your eyes than what I tell you!"

When your adored mistress has been unfaithful, reconciliation means destroying crystallization with dagger-blows, a crystallization perpetually renewing itself. Love has to die, and your heart will be rent by each wicked stage of the agony. It is one of the unhappiest relationships in love and in life, and it is better to have the strength of mind to be reconciled only as a friend.

Chapter 37 — *Roxana*

We now come to consider jealousy in women. They are mistrustful, for they are risking infinitely more than we are, and they have sacrificed more for love's sake; they have less to occupy their minds, and above all far less chance of inspecting their lover's actions. A woman feels degraded by jealousy, for it looks as though she is running after a man; she thinks her lover must be laughing at her and mocking her tenderest emotions. She must feel an urge to be cruel, and yet cannot legally kill her rival.

For women, then, jealousy must hurt even more abominably than for men, if that be possible; its impotent rage and self-contempt[87] are as much as the human heart can bear without breaking.

I see no cure for such crippling suffering except the death either of the one who inspires it or of the one who feels it. For an example of French jealousy see the story of Madame de la Pommeraie in Diderot's *Jacques-le-Fataliste*.

La Rochefoucauld says:

"We are ashamed to admit that we are jealous, yet we pride ourselves on having been jealous, and on being capable of jealousy."[88]

Women, poor things, dare not even admit that they suffer this cruel torment, for it makes them look ridiculous, and with so deep a wound they can never quite heal.

If cold reason could stanch the fire of imagination with the shadow of a chance of success, I should say to those unfortunate women tormented by jealousy:

"There is a great deal of difference between men's

unfaithfulness and yours. In your case it is partly a *direct action,* and partly *symptomatic.* Because of our military-academy type of education, it signifies nothing in a man. Because of modesty, however, it is the most decisive of all the symptoms of a woman's degree of care. Evil habits make it more or less a necessity for men. Throughout our early youth we follow the example of the so-called *bloods* of the school and take a pride in the number of our successes in this field, regarding them as proof of our merit. Your own education works in the opposite direction."

I am trying to write history, and thoughts like these are facts.

To illustrate what I mean by the *symptomatic* value of an action, let us suppose that in an angry moment I upset a table on my neighbor's foot. It will hurt him like the devil, but matters are easily mended. But, if I so much as raise my hand to strike him ...

A man's unfaithfulness is so different from a woman's that a woman in love can forgive an infidelity, but for a man this is quite impossible.

Here is a conclusive way of seeing whether a woman's love springs from passion or *pique:* unfaithfulness practically kills passion, yet it makes the latter twice as strong.

Spirited women hide their jealousy under haughty

pride, and will spend long evenings in icy silence beside the man they adore, whom they tremble to lose, and in whose eyes they think themselves unattractive. It must be torture for them, and is certainly one of the most fruitful sources of unhappiness in love. To cure a tortured woman, who so much needs our respect, we must take a delicate and precise step without appearing to recognize what is happening, such as starting on a long journey with her at twenty-four hours' notice.

Chapter 38 — About Wounded Self-Esteem

Pique[89] is a stirring of one's vanity. You do not wish your rival to get the better of you, yet *you select him as the referee and judge of your merit.* You want to make an impression on him and so go far beyond the bounds of reasonable behavior. To justify your own extravagance, sometimes you go so far as to accuse your opponent of making fun of you.

Since *pique* is a *disease of honor* it is most prevalent in monarchies and must be less so in countries where actions are habitually judged by their degree of usefulness, such as the United States of America.

Every man, not least a Frenchman, hates to be taken for a dupe. Nevertheless, under the old French monarchy,[90] with its light-hearted looseness of character, *pique* could only play havoc with mannered love and gallantry. It was only in monarchies like Portugal or Piedmont, climatically conducive to somberness of character, that pique produced really foul enormities.

The French provincial conceives a ridiculous image of what society expects in a gentleman and then spends all his life watching to see whether anyone breaks the rules. As a result, he never acts naturally and is always afflicted with pique, which makes even his love ridiculous.

Next to envy, this is the most unbearable thing about life in small towns, and it is wise to remember this when you admire some of their picturesque surroundings. The most generous and noble emotions are paralyzed by contact with the meanest products of civilization. The people in these small towns succeed in making themselves insufferable by their perennial talk of the corruption in great cities.[91]

Pique has no place in passionate love; either it is feminine pride:

"If I let my lover treat me badly he will despise me and no longer love me," or else it is sheer furious jealousy.

Jealousy wishes the death of the rival it fears. A man suffering from pique, on the other hand, wants his enemy to live and above all to witness his triumph. He would be loath to see his rival give up the contest, because the rival might be insolent enough to think: "... if I had cared to pursue the struggle I should have got the better of him..."

Pique is not in the least concerned with achieving its apparent goal, but purely with the need for victory. This is well illustrated by the love-affairs of the Opera girls; their so-called passion, that was enough to drive them to suicide, dies the moment their rivals are sent packing.

Unlike passionate love, love through pique dissolves in a moment. It only lasts until the rival admits defeat in some sound way. I am a little hesitant to put forward this statement, since I have only one example to support it, and I am not too sure even of that. Still here are the facts, which the reader may judge for himself.

Dona Diana was a young woman of twenty-three, the daughter of one of the richest and proudest citizens of Seville. She was beyond doubt a beauty, though of an obvious type, and she was credited with much intelligence and still more pride. She was passionately in love, to all appearances, with a young officer of whom her family disapproved. This young man went to America with Morillo, and they were forever writing letters to each other. One day at her mother's house, in front of a crowd of people, some idiot announced that the charming young man was dead. All eyes quickly turned upon her, but Dona Diana merely said: "What a pity-so young."

That very day we had read an old play by Massinger which ended tragically, but in which the heroine was outwardly unmoved by the news of her lover's death. I saw the mother shudder despite her pride and hatred; the father left the room to conceal his joy. In the midst of all this, while the confused spectators scowled at the idiot tattler, Dona Diana, alone and unmoved, continued conversing as if nothing had happened. Her mother was frightened and had her daughter watched by a lady's-maid, but there was no apparent change in her behavior.

Two years later, a very handsome young man paid court to Dona Diana. Once again, and for the same reason, that the suitor was not wellborn, her parents opposed the match. Dona Diana insisted that she would marry him. She and her father each piqued the other's self-esteem, and the young man was forbidden to enter the house. Dona Diana was no longer taken into the country and hardly ever to church; every possible means of meeting her lover was carefully denied her. To all this, the lover used to disguise himself, seeing her in secret, but only at long intervals. Dona Diana became increasingly obstinate, refusing the most brilliant matches, even a title and a high position at the court of Ferdinand VII.

The misfortunes of the two lovers and their heroic loyalty to each other became the talk of the whole town.

At last, when Dona Diana was about to come of age, she told her father that she wanted to exercise her right to marry whoever she pleased. The family had no choice but to start arranging the marriage; but during a formal meeting between the two families, before the arrangements were half completed, the young man broke their engagement, after being constant for six years.[92]

A quarter of an hour later Dona Diana showed no sign that anything had happened; her heart was mended. Was she in love from pique? Or was she great enough to disdain making a public exhibition of her sorrow?

Passionate love can often reach what I might call happiness only by wounding the beloved's self-esteem. A man thus appears to obtain his heart's desire, so that to complain would seem not only ridiculous but also unjustified. He cannot admit that he is unhappy, and yet he is continually prodding and testing his unhappiness; the proofs of it are, so to say, entwined in situations which are both flattering and likely to foster illusions of delight. It is an unhappiness which rears its ugly head at the tenderest moments as if to taunt the lover by showing him, on one hand, the full happiness of being loved by the charming unresponsive creature in his arms and, on the other, that this happiness can never be his. It is perhaps, after jealousy, the cruelest unhappiness of all.

There is a great city[93] where people still remember a gentle, sensitive man, afflicted with fury of this kind, who killed his mistress because she only loved him through pique against her sister. Having persuaded her to go rowing with him one evening, alone, in a pretty little boat which he had designed himself, after reaching the open sea he touched a spring; the boat sprang a great leak and sank without trace.

I have seen a man of sixty set out to keep the most capricious, irresponsible, lovable, and marvelous actress on the London stage—Miss Cornel.

"And you think she will be faithful to you?" he was asked.

"Nor in the least," he replied, "but she will love me, even wildly for that matter."

She did love him, for a whole year, and frequently to distraction; for as long as three consecutive months she gave him no cause for complaint. He had established a state of pique, by quite shocking means, between his mistress and her daughter.

In mannered love pique definitely triumphs, since it shapes the whole course of events. It is the best test for distinguishing between mannered and passionate love. Every recruit must have heard the old soldier's proverb that if you are billeted in a house where two sisters live, and you want one of them to love you, you must make eyes at the other one. Generally speaking, among young and willing Spanish women, all you need do is advertise modestly how little interested you are in the particular lady of the house. I got this useful tip from my good friend General Lasalle. On the other hand, it may be the most dangerous way of tackling passionate love.

A state of pique can produce the happiest marriages, second only to love matches. Husbands frequently make sure of the love of their wives for many long years by taking a little mistress two months after their marriage.[94] The wives are thus induced to form the habit of confining their thoughts to one man until family ties ensue to make this habit unbreakable.

In the time of Louis XV there was only one reason why a great lady at his court (Madame de Choiscul) was known to adore her husband:[95] he seemed to be extremely fond of her sister, the Duchesse de Gramont.

The most neglected mistress —once she shows a preference for another man— will rob us of all peace, stirring our hearts into something that is much like passion.

The courage of an Italian is a fit of anger, that of a German a moment of intoxication, and of a Spaniard an expression of pride.

If there were a nation where courage took the form of a

pique of self-esteem between the soldiers of each company and between the regiments of each division, it'd be impossible to halt the retreat of such an army if it were once put to rout, without strong support positions in the rear. To foresee the danger and attempt to avert it would be futile with such vainglorious runaways.

"Any account of a journey among the savages of North America," writes one of the most delightful of French philosophers,[96] 'will be sure to relate the normal fate of prisoners of war. Not only are they burned alive and eaten, but they are first tied to a stake near flaming logs and tortured for several hours by the most ferocious and refined methods which hatred can imagine. It is worth reading the travelers' accounts of the cannibal joy of those who take part in these frightful scenes, particularly of the fury of the women and children, and their atrocious pleasure as they compete with one another in cruelty.

It is worth seeing what they say about the heroic resilience and cool self-control shown by the prisoners who, besides betraying no pain, even taunt and defy their executioners with the haughtiest pride, the bitterest irony and the most insulting sarcasm: they sing their own feats, and name the spectators' relatives and friends whom they have killed, detailing the tortures they inflicted. They accuse all around them of cowardice, weakness, and incompetence as torturers. In the end, torn to ribbons, eaten alive before their own eyes by their frenzied enemies, their voices quaver with a last insult as they die.[97] All this will hardly be believed by civilized nations; our bravest Grenadier captains will regard it as a myth, and posterity will one day question it."

This physiological phenomenon results from a particular state of mind in which the prisoner undertakes a battle of self-esteem between himself and his torturers. This is a challenge of vanity against vanity as to who can hold out longest.

Our excellent army surgeons have often noticed that casualties who, had their minds and senses been normal, would have screamed during surgery, in fact displayed calm strength of character when they were suitably prepared. They had to have their honor impugned; it had to be asserted, at first tentatively and then with annoying insistence, that they were not able to bear the operation without screaming.

Chapter 39 — (I): Love at Loggerheads

Love quarrels are of two kinds:

1. When the one who starts the quarrel is in love.

2. When the quarreler is not in love.

Where one of the lovers holds too much advantage over

the other in certain qualities which they both value, the other's love will die because sooner or later fear of contempt will abruptly stop the process of crystallization.

Nothing is more hateful to mediocre people than intellectual superiority in others. In our society it is the very fountainhead of hatred. If this fact does not breed atrocious hatreds it is only because the people divided thereby are not obliged to live together. But consider what happens in love where natural behavior is not masked and where the superior partner, in particular, does not conceal his superiority behind social wariness.

If the passion is to survive, the inferior lover must ill-treat the other, who will otherwise be unable even to close a window without giving offence.

As a superior lover you will create illusions, and not only will your love run no risks, but the very weakness of your beloved will strengthen the bond between the two of you.

Judging by sheer durability, passionate requited love between people of the same caliber takes first place.

Love at loggerhead, where the quarreler does not love, comes a close second. You will find examples of this in stories about the Duchesse de Berry in the *Memoirs* of Duclos. This kind of love, given the coldness of habit, springing from the prosaic and selfish parts of life which follow a man to his grave, may last longer than passionate love itself.

In fact it is no longer love but merely a habit caused by love, whose only relation to the original passion is one of memories and physical pleasure. The existence of this habit necessarily presupposes natures of lesser nobility. Every day some little crisis may occur:

"Will he scold me...?" which, as in passionate love, keeps the imagination busy; and every day some new proof of tenderness has to be given. See the anecdotes about Mme d'Houdetot and Saint-Lambert.[98]

Occasionally pride may refuse to stoop to this sort of thing; then, after a few stormy months, pride kills love. But you will find that the nobler passion makes prolonged resistance before it succumbs.

A lover who is still in love, despite ill-treatment, will long continue to foster an illusion about 'little tiffs'. A few tender reconciliations can help to make, the transition bearable. On the plea of some secret sorrow or stroke of ill-luck, you forgive the person you have loved so much, becoming in the end accustomed to a cat-and-dog life.

After all, excluding passionate love, gambling, and the enjoyment of power,[99] where would you find so rich a source of daily interest? If the aggressor dies, you will notice that the surviving victim is inconsolable. This standard is the successful basis of many middle-class marriages; the scolded ones have to listen all day to their favorite topic.

There exists also a kind of love that is pseudo-quarrelsome. I have borrowed my Chapter 33 from the letter of an extremely clever woman:

"Always a little doubt to set at rest — that's what keeps one craving in passionate love. Because the keenest misgivings are always there, its pleasures never become tedious."

With boorish, ill-bred, or very violent people, this little doubt to be set at rest, this slight anxiety, takes the form of a quarrel.

Unless the beloved owns that extreme subtlety which results from a careful upbringing, she may find this kind of love more lively, and therefore more enjoyable; and however fastidious she may be she will find it very difficult, when she sees *her furious* lover the first to suffer from his own violent emotions, not to love him the more for it. Perhaps what Lord Mortimer misses most about his mistress are the candlesticks she used to throw at his head. Indeed, if pride will pardon and allow sensations such as these, it must be admitted that they wage a bitter war against boredom, which is the great affliction of contented people.

Saint-Simon, the only historian France has ever possessed, says:

"After many passing fancies the Duchesse de Berry had fallen deeply in love with Riom, a junior member of the d'Aydie family, the son of one of Madame de Biron's sisters. He had neither looks nor brains; he was fat, short, chubby-cheeked, and pale, and had such a crop of pimples that he seemed one large abscess; he had beautiful teeth, but not the least idea that he was going to inspire a passion which quickly got out of control, a passion which lasted a lifetime, despite the number of subsidiary flirtations and affairs. He didn't have a penny to bless himself with, and his numerous brothers and sisters were just as poor as he. The Duchess's tirewoman and her husband, Mme and M. de Pons, were related to them, coming from the same part of the country. Hoping to make something of the young man, who was then a lieutenant in the dragoons, they invited him to stay with them. No sooner had he arrived than he took the Duchess's fancy and became master in the Luxembourg.

"M. de Lauzun, whose great-nephew he was, laughed up his sleeve about all this. He was overjoyed, and in the young man saw himself all over again, as he used to be at the Luxembourg in the days of the great Mademoiselle. He used to advise the boy what to do, and Riom, who was naturally gentle, polite, and respectful, paid heed to him like the honest lad he was. But very soon he grew aware of the power his charms conferred, with their unique appeal to the loose fancy of the princess. He did not exercise this power unfairly over others, thus becoming popular with everyone, though he used to treat his duchess as M. de Lauzun had treated Mademoiselle. He was soon attired in the richest lace and the finest garments, and provided with money, jewelry, and buckles. He would excite but not stir deeply the desire of the princess, delighting in making her jealous or pretending to be jealous himself. He would often drive her to tears. Slowly he forced her into the position of doing nothing without his leave, even trifles of no importance. Sometimes, when she was ready to go to the Opera, he insisted that she stay at home; and sometimes he made her go there against her will. He compelled her to grant favors to ladies she did not like or of whom she was jealous, and to deny favors to people she did like, of whom he pretended to be jealous. She was not even free to dress as she chose. He would amuse himself by making her change her coiffure or her dress at the last minute, going this so often and so publicly that she became used to taking his orders in the evening for what she would do and wear the following day. Then the next day he would change everything, and the princess would cry all the more. In the end she took to sending him messages by trusted footmen, for from the first he had taken up residence in the Luxembourg; messages which continued throughout her toilette, to know what ribbons she would wear, what gown and what other ornaments. Invariably he made her wear something she did not wish to. When she occasionally dared to do anything, however small, without his leave, he treated her like a servant, and she was in tears for several days.

"This proud princess, whose pleasure was to behave with the greatest arrogance, was demeaned herself to attend obscure dinners with him among a crowd of ne'er-do-wells; indeed this very woman with whom no one was permitted to sit at table unless he was a prince of the blood. Riglet, a Jesuit whom she had known as a child and who cultivated her, was invited to these private dinner-parties, without shame or mortification on either side. Madame de Mouchy was privy to all the strange goings-on; she and Riom would invite the guests and name the days, and she used to patch up the lovers' quarrels.

All this was common knowledge in the Luxembourg, where Riom was sought after by everyone.

As for him, he took care to be on good terms with everybody, behaving to all others with a respect which he publicly denied only to his princess. Right in front of the assembled company he would give her such brutal replies that made everyone lower their eyes, and the Duchess would blush, yet her passion for him was in no way diminished."

For the princess, Riom was a sovereign remedy against boredom.

When Bonaparte was a young hero covered with glory and still innocent of any crime against liberty, a famous woman suddenly blurted out to him:

"General, a woman must be either your wife or your sister!'" The hero did not understand the compliment, which brought some fine insults upon his head. Women of this kind love to be despised by their lovers and can only love cruel men.

Chapter 39 — 9 (ii) *Cures for Love*

In olden times the Leucadian Leap was an apt image. It is really almost impossible to find a cure for love. Not only must there be danger, to remind a man forcibly of the need for self-preservation,[100] but, and this is much more difficult to find, it must be a relentless pressing danger, yet one which a man can skillfully avoid for long enough to reacquire the habit of thinking about the need for survival. In my opinion nothing less than a sixteen-day storm as in Don Juan,[101] or M. Cochelet's shipwreck among the Moors will suffice; otherwise you very soon become inured to danger, and in the front line, twenty paces from the enemy, you again begin thinking of your beloved even more devotedly than ever.

We have reiterated often enough that when a man really loves he *rejoices* or *trembles* no matter what he thinks about, with everything in nature speaking to him of his beloved. Now rejoicing and trembling are interesting activities beside which all others pale.

A friend who wishes to cure lovesickness must in the first place always be on the side of the beloved woman, and yet friends with more zeal than shrewdness never fail to do the opposite. This is simply to attack, with inanely weak forces, that pattern of exquisite illusion which we have already called crystallization.[102]

The healing friend must always keep in mind that where the lover has a choice between swallowing some absurdity or giving up all that makes life worth living, he will swallow it and use all his smarts to disprove his mistress's most obvious vices and most blatant infidelities. This is how in passionate love everything is forgiven after a little while.

Men of cold calculating temperament will only accept vices in their mistresses after several months of passion.[103]

Rather than seeking crudely and openly to amuse the lover, the healing friend should talk to him *ad nauseam* about both his love and his mistress, while contriving a series of trivial events around him. If travel *isolates* it is no cure,[104] and indeed nothing is more tenderly reminiscent of the beloved than changes of scene. In brilliant Paris salons, among the reputedly most charming women, I have felt the greatest love for my own poor mistress, solitary and sad in her little lodging in the depths of the Romagna.[105]

An exile in a splendid salon, I used to watch the magnificent clock for the exact moment when she would be leaving her lodging on foot, even in the rain, to visit her friend. In seeking to forget her I discovered that changes of scene provided memories, less vivid but far more sublime than those aroused by places where we had once met.

For absence to be of any use, the healing friend must always be on hand to keep chatting as much as possible on the events which have taken place in the love affair, ensuring that these reflections are long, wearisome, and pointless, so that they begin to sound like commonplace. Tender sentimentality, for example, could be used after a dinner party enlivened with good wines.

The problem with forgetting a woman with whom you have been happy is that the imagination tirelessly continues to bring up and embellish moments of the past.

Let's say nothing about pride, a cruel though certain cure, but not one for delicate people.

The early scenes of Shakespeare's *Romeo* are an admirable illustration. It is a far cry from the man who tells himself sadly: "She hath forsworn to love" to the one who exclaims at the pinnacle of his happiness: "Come what sorrow can!"

Chapter 39 (III) — Metaphors for love

Her passion will die like a lamp for want of what the flame should feed upon.

Lammermoor, II.

The healing friend must beware of empty arguments, for example the mention of *ingratitude.* This will renew crystallization by allowing another victory and a new pleasure.

Ingratitude doesn't exist in love; the pleasure of the moment always seems worth, and more than worth, the utmost sacrifice. The only thing that can be seen as wrong is a lack of frankness; one *must* be honest and open about one's heart.

To respond to even the mildest frontal attack on love, the lover will tell the healing friend "To be in love, even if your beloved is angry with you, is as good —to descend to your marketplace metaphor— as having a lottery ticket where the prize is a thousand times more desirable than anything you can offer me from your sordid world of indifference and selfish interests.

"To be happy just because you are well-received shows a great deal of vanity, of the small-minded vanity at that. I don't censure men for acting that way in their world. But with Leonore I discovered a world where things were heavenly, tender, and generous. The most sublime and almost unbelievable virtue of your world would have been no more, in our conversations, than a commonplace every day virtue. At least let me dream of the happiness of spending mv life with such a being. Although I realize I have been betrayed by calumny, and have no more hope, at least I can forgo my revenge for her sake."

It is almost useless trying to stop love except in its very early stages.

Besides immediate departure, and the compulsory distractions of high society, as in the case of Countess Kalemberg, there are several other little tricks which the healing friend can bring into play. For example, he can draw to your attention, apparently quite by chance, that the woman you love does not, in matters irrelevant to the main issue, give you the politeness and respect she gave your rival. The most trivial things will suffice, for in love everything is a *symbol*. Perhaps she does not give you her arm when at the theatre you escort her to her box; a trifle like this, taken in tragic earnest by a passionate heart, by joining a humiliation to every judgment which crystallization makes, poisons the very source of love and may destroy it.

The unkind woman may be accused of some humiliating physical defect which it is impossible to verify; if the calumny could be verified and found true it would very soon be disposed of by the imagination, and forgotten. It is only imagination that can resist imagination, as Henry III well knew when he spoke ill of the celebrated Duchesse de Montpensier.

Above anything else, we must control the imagination in a girl if you wish to save her from love. The less commonplace her spirit the more noble and generous her nature; in short, the more worthy she is of our respect the greater the risk she runs.

It is always dangerous for a young woman to allow her recollections to dwell too often and too easily upon any one person. If the ties of memory get strengthened by gratitude, admiration, or curiosity, she is almost certainly on the edge of the precipice. The greater the tedium of her daily life the more deadly will be the poisons called gratitude, admiration, and curiosity. Immediate, swift, and energetic distractions then become necessary.

It's clear then that small doses of roughness and unconcern at the beginning —provided the drug be administered in simple manner— are infallible means of getting the respect of an intelligent woman.

---

[1] "Cut out this bit," they tell me, "it's perfectly true, but watch out for businessmen; they will cry 'aristocrat!'" I was not afraid of the Procurator-General in 1817, so why should I fear millionaires in 1826? The ships sold to the Pasha of Egypt have opened my eyes to *their* little game, and I only fear what I respect.

[2] A known conversation between Pont de Veyle and Mme du Deffand, by the fireside.

[3] This book is freely translated from an Italian manuscript by M. Lisio Visconti, a prominent young man, who has just died at his home in Volterra. On the day of his unexpected death he gave the translator permission to publish his essay on Love, if a way could be found of reducing it to a proper form. Castel Fiorentino, 10th June 1819.

[4] If men do not display this peculiarity, it is because they have no modesty to sacrifice.

[5] This means that the same subtlety of existence provides only one moment of perfect happiness; but the passionate man's *manner of being* changes ten times a day.

[6] What the seventeenth-century novelists called the *'coup de foudre'* (or thunderbolt), which determines the fate of the hero and his mistress, is a motion in the soul which, for all its sullying by a thousand scribblers, is none the less a fact of nature. It comes from the impossibility of performing this defensive maneuver. A woman in love finds so much happiness in the feelings she is experiencing that she cannot pretend; tired of being prudent, she throws caution

to the wind, flinging herself blindly into the happiness of loving. Where there is mistrust there can be no *coup deoudre.*

[7] I have called this essay a book of ideology, meaning that although it was about *love,* it was not a novel, and was not entertaining in the way that a novel is. I beg the forgiveness of the philosophers for having chosen the word *ideology.* I surely did not intend stealing a title that rightly belongs to someone else. If ideology is a detailed description of ideas and of all the parts into which those ideas can be analyzed, this book is a detailed and painful description of all the feelings which make up the passion called *love.* I then draw certain conclusions from this description; for instance, the way in which love can be cured. I know of no word derived from Greek that would indicate discourse upon feelings, as ideology indicates discourse upon ideas. I might have had a word invented for me by one of my scholarly friends, but I am already quite vexed enough having had to adopt the new word *crystallization,* and it may well be that if this essay wins any readers, they will not forgive me the neologism. I agree that literary talent would have avoided it and I tried to do so, but without any success. I think this word expresses the main process of the illness known as love, a madness which provides man with the grandest pleasures the species can know on earth. If I had not used the word *crystallization* I should have had to replace it repeatedly by an awkward periphrasis, and my description of what happens in the head and in the heart of a man in love would have become opaque, heavy, and tedious even to me, the author. I hesitate to guess what the reader would have thought of it.

I therefore ask anyone who is shocked by the word *crystallization* to close the book right away. I don't wish, fortunately, to have a great number of readers. It would make me very happy to please about thirty or forty people in Paris, whom I shall never see but nevertheless love devotedly without ever having met them: some young Madame Roland, for instance, surreptitiously reading a volume which she thrusts into a drawer at the slightest noise, by the workbench in the back of her father's watch-engraving shop. Someone like Madame Roland will, I hope, forgive me not only the word *crystallization,*—which I use to express the impulse of folly that makes us see all beauties and perfections in the woman we are beginning to love— but also many bolder ellipses. The only thing to do is to take a pencil and write in the few missing words between the lines.

[8] To be brief, and in order to depict experience from the inside, that the author, by using the first person singular, brings together a number of feelings quite alien to him. He has had none of his own which are worth mentioning.

[9] At first all these actions seemed to me to have the sublimity that at once sets a man apart, distinguishing him from all others. I thought I saw in his eyes that thirst for more sublime happiness, that unsung melancholy which aspires to something better than we can know here below, and which, for a romantic soul, however placed by chance or revolution,... *Still prompts the celestial sight, for which we wish to live, or dare to die.(Ultima lettera di Biatica a sua madre.* Forli, 1817).

[10] As far as crime is concerned, a good education instills remorse; and foreseen remorse acts as a deterrent.

[11] Diane de Poitiers, in the *Princesse de Cleves.*

[12] If you could imagine happiness there, crystallization would have claimed for your mistress the exclusive right to give you *that* happiness.

[13] This second crystallization does not occur in women of easy virtue, who are far removed from such romantic ideas.

[14] Epicurus: discrimination is a must to the achievement of pleasure.

[15] Compare the maxim of Beaumarchais: Nature says to a woman, "If you can, be beautiful; if you like, be wise; but whatever happens, be respected." In France, no respect means no admiration and therefore no love.

[16] *Quando legemmo il disiato riso*
Esser baciato da cotanto amante,
Questi che mai da me non fia diuiso,
La bocca mi bacio tutto tremante.
Francesca da Rimini, Dante.

[17] *Empoli,* June 1819.

[18] "Those who remarked in the countenance of this young hero a dissolute
audacity mingled with extreme haughtiness and indifference to the feelings of
others, could not yet deny to his countenance that sort of comeliness which
belongs to an open set of features, well formed by nature, modelled by art to
the usual rules of courtesy, yet so far frank and honest that they seemed as if they
disclaimed to conceal the natural working of the soul. Such an expression is
often mistaken for *manly frankness,* when in truth it arises from the reckless
indifference of a libertine disposition, conscious *of superiority of birth, of wealth,*
or of some other adventitious advantage totally unconnected with personal
merit."   *Ivanhoe,* **Volume i, p. 145.**

[19] *Beauty,* as I intend it here, means the promise of a quality useful to my soul, and transcends physical attraction; the latter being of only one particular kind. 1815.

[20] There is a physical cause, an incipient madness, a rush of blood to the brain, a disorder of the nervous system and the cerebral centers; compare the fleeting courage shown by stags and the color of a soprano's thoughts. In 1922, physiology will provide us with a description of the physical basis of this phenomenon. I recommend it to the attention of Mr Edwards.

[21] Hence passions may be of artificial origin; and like that of Benedick and Beatrice (Shakespeare).

[22] cf. the Loves of Struenzee in *The Courts of the North,* by Brown, 3 vols. 1819.

[23] See the *Letters* of Madame du Deffand and of Mademoiselle de Lespinasse, the *Memoirs* of Bczcnval, of Lauzun, and of Madame d'Epinay, *le Dictionnaire des Etiquettes* by Madame de Gcnlis, the *Memoirs* of Dangeau and of Horace Walpole.

[24] Unless it be at the court of St Petersburg.

[25] See Saint-Simon and *Werther.* However sensitive and fastidious a solitary man may be, he is distracted, and part of his imagination is engaged in anticipating society. Force of character is one of the charms which most appeals to the truly feminine; hence the success of very serious young officers. Women are very clever at telling between strength of character and the violence of passions, which they themselves feel potentially in their hearts. The finest women are sometimes taken in by a little charlatanism of that kind. This can be used quite safely as soon as crystallization is seen to be well under way.

[26] Scents.

[27] See note 2 on p. 49.

[28] ... *Nessun maggiot dolore*
Che ricordarsi del tempo felice
Nella miseria
Dante, *Francesco*

[29] I have been advised in the first place to do away with this word, or, if I cannot do that, to include frequent reminders that by *crystallization* I mean a certain fever of the imagination which translates a normally commonplace object into something unrecognizable, and makes it an entity apart. Among those who can only achieve happiness through vanity, the man who wishes to excite this fever must take great pains with his cravat and be constantly on the watch over a thousand details, none of which must be neglected. Women in society admit the effect and at the same time deny, or fail to see, the cause.

[30] Copied from Lisio's journal.

[31] *Othello* and *The Vestal,* ballets by Vigano, danced by La Pallerini and Molinari.

[32] Beauty is only the promise of happiness. The happiness of a Greek differed from the happiness of a Frenchman in 1822. Consider the eyes of the Medici Venus, and compare them with those of the Magdalen of Pordenone (at M. de Sommariva's).

[33] If one is sure of a woman's love, one looks to see whether she is beautiful or not; if one is doubtful of her heart, there is no time to inspect her face.

[34] cf. Mine dc Stael, in *Delphine,* I believe. This is the artifice of plain women.

[35] It is to this nervous sympathy that I am tempted to attribute the prodigious and unaccountable effect of

fashionable music (at Dresden, for Rossini, 1821). As soon as it is out of fashion —and it is none the worse for that— it no longer has any effect on the guileless hearts of young girls. It may have appealed to them because it stirred the emotions of young men. *Miserere* was still more augmented, and there was a *Libera* that filled all eyes with tears.'
One can no more doubt the truth of this effect than question Mme de SeVigne's intelligence or subtlety. The Lully music that delighted her would frighten people away nowadays. At that time such music encouraged crystallization, but today it makes crystallization impossible.

[36] This is the advantage of being in fashion. Setting aside the facial defects already known which no longer stimulate the imagination, one focuses on one of the three following kinds of beauty:
1. Among the common people: the idea of wealth;
2. In society: the idea of material or moral elegance;
3. At Court: the idea 'I want to please the ladies.'

Almost everywhere there is a mixture of these three ideas. The happiness associated with the idea of wealth combines with the subtle pleasures which derive from the idea of elegance, and the whole is applied to love. In one way or another imagination reacts enthusiastically to what is new. Thus a woman can become interested in a very ugly man without noticing his ugliness, and in the long run his ugliness becomes beauty. Madame Vigano, a dancer and the fashionable woman of the day in 1788, was pregnant, and very soon the ladies began to sport little tummies *a la Vigano.* By the same reasoning in reverse, there is nothing so terrifying as an outmoded fashion. Bad taste consists in confusing fashion, which survives by change, with lasting beauty which is the outcome of such and such a government in such and such a climate. A 'fashionable' building is out of date in ten years' time. It will be less displeasing two hundred years later when the fashion has been forgotten. Lovers are quite crazy to think about dressing well; when one meets the beloved there are many things to do besides thinking about her toilette. As Rousseau says, you look at your lover, you don't examine her. If examination does occur, it is no longer a case of passionate love but of mannered love. Beauty which dazzles is almost offensive in the one you love; you are not concerned with her beauty but wish to see her tender and languishing. In love, fine clothes only make a difference in the case of young girls, who, because strictly confined to their fathers' houses, often reach passion only through the eyes.

Remarks by L., 15th September 1820.

Little Jermyn, in the *Memoirs* of Grammont.

[37] Either for their polish, or their size, or their shape. It is in this way, or by
the association of feelings (see above, concerning smallpox scars) that a woman
in love becomes accustomed to ignore the defects of her lover. The Russian princess C.
has become quite used to a man who, to put it bluntly, has no nose. This
miracle has been wrought by a mental picture of courage, of a loaded pistol
ready for suicide in despair at this misfortune, combined with pity at the depth
of the disaster and the idea that he will recover - that, in fact, he had already
begun to recover. Berlin, 1807.

[38] An unseemly phrase, copied from the *Memoirs* of my good friend the late Baron de Bottmer. It is by the same artifice that Feramorz pleased Lalla-Rookh; see this delightful poem.

[39] Clearly the author is neither prince nor millionaire. I did not wish the reader to think of this remark before I did!

[40] Miss Ashton, the Bride of Lammermoor. A man of experience will have more memories *of loves* than he can choose from. But as soon as he wishes to write, he no longer knows which to give as examples. Anecdotes about particular communities in which he has lived are unknown to the public, and it would require a vast number of pages to narrate them with the necessary nuances. This is why I quote novels, as being universally known; but the ideas I put before the reader are based on no such empty fictions, which for the most part strive after effect rather than truth.

[41] Translated literally from Bottmer's *Memoirs*.

[42] Several sentences are borrowed from Crebillon, Vol. III.

[43] So Leonore used to say.

[44] Posen, 1807.

[45] See the travels of Bougainville, Cook, etc. The females of certain species of animals seem to withhold themselves at the very moment of surrender. We must look to comparative anatomy for the most important revelations about ourselves.

[46] Shows his love in another way.

[47] See the admirable description of this boring way of life at the end of *Corinne;* Mme de Stael has dealt more than kindly with it.

[48] Both the Bible and the aristocracy take a cruel revenge on those who believe they owe everything to them.

[49] I am told to withhold this detail. "You must think me an extremely light woman, to dare tell me such things."

[50] Modesty is one of the sources of good taste in dress; a woman promises either more or less by some slight

arrangement of it. That is why fine clothes are out of place when a woman is no longer young.

A woman from the provinces, if she attempts to follow Paris fashions, seems pretentious and laughable. When she first arrives in Paris she should start by dressing as if she were thirty.

[51] Compare the tone of society in Geneva, particularly among the *best* families; function of a Court to counteract by ridicule any prudish tendencies; Duclos telling stories to Mme de Rochefort: 'Really, you think us women much more respectable than we are!' There is nothing more boring than false modesty.

[52] Really, my dear Fronsac, the story you're beginning is twenty bottles ahead of what we're talking about now.

[53] It is a question of the melancholic temperament as compared with the sanguine: look at a virtuous woman, even one whose virtue is of the business kind as opposed by religions (which promise to repay virtue a hundredfold in Paradise), and at a jaded old rogue of forty. Although Valmont in *Les Liaisons Dangereuses* has not yet reached that stage, the Presidentc de Tourvel is happier than he is, throughout the novel; and if the clever author had been cleverer still, that would have been the moral of his ingenious work.

[54] *The Heart of Midlothian,* Vol. m.

[55] Monarchy without Charter or Parliament.

[56] Alas, when you return to the world of the living, remember me. I am Pia; Siena gave me life, and I found death in the Maremma. He who gave me his ring in marriage knows my story.

[57] I always return from visiting Miss Cornel full of admiration and deep thoughts about passion in the raw. She has an

imperious way of giving orders to her servants; not that she is despotic but the result of a clear and swift appraisal of what has to be done. Angry with me at the beginning of my visit, she has forgotten all about it by the end. She explains the whole pattern of her passion for Mortimer: "I like meeting him in company much better than alone." A woman of the greatest genius could do no more, because she dares to be perfectly *natural* and is not hampered by theories: "I am happier as an actress than I would be married to a peer." A great woman, whose friendship I must cherish for my own edification.

[58] Hauteur and courage in little things, but a passionate regard for those little things; the strength of the bilious temperament; his conduct with Madame de Monaco (Saint-Simon, v. 383); his escapade beneath Madame de Montespan's bed, when the king was with her. Without a regard for little things, this kind of character cannot be grasped by women.

[59] When Minna Toil Heard a tale of woe or of romance, it was then her blood rushed to her cheeks, and showed plainly how warm it beat despite the generally serious, composed and retiring disposition which her countenance and demeanor seemed to exhibit (The Pirate, I. 33).

[60] Mary Stuart, speaking of Leicester, after her fatal interview with Elizabeth.

[61] It is common knowledge that this celebrated woman, with M. de la Rochefoucauld, lived the story of La *Princesse de Cleves* in real life, and that the two authors passed the last twenty years of their lives together in perfect friendship. This is exactly love *a I'ltalienne.*

[62] *Sotto I'usbergo del sentirsi pura.* Dante.

[63] This is something I have often thought to see in love, this

tendency to draw more misery from unhappy things than joy from happy ones.

[64] Don Carlos, Saint-Preux, and Hippolyte and Bajazet in Racine.

[65] Mordaunt Merton, 1st vol. of *The Pirate.*

[66] Since I have mentioned Correggio I might say that you will find the lineaments of happy love in the head of an angel sketched on the tribune of the Florence gallery; and the downcast eyes of love in the Madonna Crowned by Jesus, at Parma.

[67] *Come what sorrow can,*
It cannot countervail the exchange of joy
That one short moment gives me in her sight.
Romeo and Juliet.

[68] A few days before he died he wrote an ode which has the merit of expressing the precise feelings about which he had been telling us:

L'ULTIMO DI anacreontica A ELVIRA

Vedi tu dove il rio

Lambendo un mirto va,

La del riposo mio

La pietra surgera.   .

Il passero amoroso,

E il nobile usignuol,

Entro quel mirto ombroso

Raccoglieranno il vol.

Odi d'un uom che muore

Odi l'estremo suon

Questo appassito fiore

Ti lascio, Elvira, in don

Quanto prezioso ei sia

Saper tu il devi appien;

Il di che fosti mia,

Te l'involai dal sen.

[69] Miserable wretch! How sweet his thoughts and how constant his desire until his last hour. He was handsome, with a fine and gentle face, except for a noble scar which broke the line of an eyebrow.

[70] *Vie de Haydn,* p. 228.

[71] 20th September 1811.

[72] This kind of shyness is conclusive proof of passionate love in a man of intelligence.

[73] A reminder that if the author on occasion uses the first person singular, it is in an attempt to bring some variety into the form of this essay. He has no intention whatsoever of inflicting his own private feelings upon his readers. He seeks to impart with as little monotony as possible what he has observed in other people.

[74] This will depend upon the same actions.

[75] *Hoec autem at acerbam rei memoriam amara dulcedine scribere visum est... ut*
cogitem nihil esse debere quod amplius mini placed in hac vita.
15th January 1819, Petrarch. Marsand's edition.

[76] Venice, 1819.

[77] *Memoirs* of Madame d'Epinay, Geliotte.
Prague, Klagenfurt, the whole of Moravia, etc., etc. The women there are extremely witty and the men keen hunters. Friendship between women is very common. Winter is the best season there; hunting parties lasting a fortnight or three weeks follow each other at the mansions of the great lords of the province. One of the wittiest of them once told me that since Charles V had been the lawful ruler of all Italy, there was absolutely no point in the Italians trying to rebel. The wife of this noble gentleman used to read the *Letters* of Mile de Lespinasse.
Znaym, 1816.

[78] A moot point. It seems to me that besides education, which begins at the age of eight or nine months, there is a certain degree of instinct.

[79] We find descriptions of physical love in the Venetian dialect which leave Horace, Propertius, La Fontaine, and all the poets miles behind. M. Burati, of Venice, is now the leading satirical poet in the whole of our sad Europe. He is particularly adept at describing the grotesque physical appearance of his heroes. He is also often in prison; see his *Elefanteide, Uomo,* and *Strejeide.*

[80] This is part of love's folly, for the perfection one can see is not a perfection to him.

[81] Montagnola, 13th April 1819.

[82] *La Princesse de Tarente,* a short story by Scarron.

[83] As in *Le Curieux Impertinent,* a short story by Cervantes.

[84] An academy should be established in Philadelphia for the exclusive purpose of gathering material for the study of man in

a state of nature. This should be done now, before these strange tribes become extinct.

I know there are such academies, but apparently their regulations are no better than those of our Academies in Europe. (Note and discussion on the Zodiac of Dendcrah at the Acadcmie des Sciences in Paris, in 1821.) I see that the Academy of Massachusetts, if I am not mistaken, has very prudently requested a member of the clergy, Mr Jarvis, to report on the religion of the savages. This priest eagerly and wholeheartedly refutes a godless Frenchman named Volney. According to the priest, the savages entertain the most exact and noble ideas about the Divinity, and so forth. If he lived in England a report of this kind would earn the worthy academician a preferment of several hundred pounds and the protection of every noble lord in the county. But in America.. .. ! The absurdity of this academy reminds me that free Americans set much value on seeing fine coats-of-arms painted on their carriage doors. They have, however, to contend with a lack of education among their coach-painters which leads to frequent errors in heraldry.

[85] One compares the leafless bough to the bough studded with diamonds, and the contrast enhances one's memories.

[86] For example, Alfieri's love for that great English lady (Milady Ligonicr) who also used to make love with her footman and sign herself, amusingly enough, *Penelope*. Vita, 2.

[87] This contempt is one of the chief causes of suicide. You kill yourself to avenge your honor.

[88] Thought no. 495. The reader will have observed several other thoughts from famous writers, without the necessity of my acknowledgement.

[89] *'Puntiglio'* in Italian.

[90] Three out of every four French noblemen around 1778 would have been liable to criminal conviction in a country where the laws were enforced without respect for persons.

[91] When it comes to love, they are all enviously spying on each other's activities, so that there is less love in the provinces, and more libertinage. Italy is more fortunate.

[92] Every year there are several cases where women are thrown over just as basely, and I excuse mistrust among decent women.—Mirabeau, *Lettres a Sophie.* Public opinion has no power in countries under despotic rule; all that matters is to be friends with the Pasha.

[93] Leghorn, 1819.

[94] See the confessions of a peculiar man (Mrs Opie's story).

[95] *Letters* of Madame Du Deffand; *Memoirs* of Lauzun.

[96] Volney, *Tableau des Etats-Unis d'Amerique,* pp. 491-6.

[97] Someone accustomed to such a spectacle, and who feels that he might be the hero of it, can concentrate his attention upon the nobility, whereupon the whole thing becomes the chief and most intimate of non-active pleasures.

[98] The *Memoires* of Madame d'Epinay, I think, or of Marmontel.

[99] There is also a kind of love that is pseudo-quarrelsome. I have whatever some hypocritical ministers of government may say about it, power is the greatest of all pleasures. It seems that only love can beat it, and love is a happy illness that can't be picked up as easily as a Ministry.

[100] The risk run by Henry Morton in the Clyde. *Old Mortality.* Vol. IV, p. 224.

[101] By the overrated Lord Byron.

[102] Purely for the sake of brevity, and begging forgiveness for the neologism.

[103] Madame Dornal and Serigny, in the *Confessions du Comte*, by Duclos; sec his note 4, p. 68; death of General Abdallah at Bologna.

[104] I have wept nearly every day (precious words of 10th June).

[105] Salviati.

Printed in Great Britain
by Amazon